A REGIMENT SAVED

An account of Operation Borderer
23rd July 1991 to 3rd February 1993

DONALD FAIRGRIEVE

EDINBURGH
B&W PUBLISHING
1993

First published 1993
by B&W Publishing
Edinburgh
ISBN 1 873631 28 6

British Library Cataloguing in Publication Data:
A catalogue record for this book is available from
the British Library

Cover photo © Michael Hall
All other photos © Michael Hall
Cover design Harry Palmer

Printed by Biddles Ltd, Guildford

INTRODUCTION
by
Brigadier Frank Coutts

This is a story which had to be told, and Donald Fairgrieve is just the man to tell it for he was the driving force of Operation Borderer from the very beginning - a man with a missionary gleam in his eye, who would not countenance defeat. He has made a grand job of it. The narrative runs easily from first to last.

After 43 years in uniform it was almost unthinkable that one should challenge an order - let alone take part in a "demo"! But was it a "reasonable" order? Definitely not. Mr Tom King, the Defence Secretary had a difficult task in pruning the services in order to achieve a Peace Dividend. In his so-called Options for Change he undoubtedly went too far - Treasury-driven - and he certainly hammered the Scots. What "options"? There were no options. It was a hatchet job.

Donald Fairgrieve sets down logically and fairly the reasons why Mr King's "options" were unreasonable and he proves conclusively that the campaign was not fought on sentimental, or even regimental, grounds. The defence needs of the country were the only criteria.

Donald has been excessively courteous to everyone - even to Mr King's civil servants who certainly did not merit anyone's thanks! We are used to politicians using "terminological inexactitudes" or "being economical with the truth"; when civil servants resort to these tactics, they are plain liars.

Above all, Operation Borderer was a total justification of the regimental system with every member of the family doing his or her bit for the cause. But not in isolation. All policies were co-ordinated by the splendid "Keep Our Scottish Battalions" committee chaired by Lt General Sir John MacMillan and to them must go the major credit for winning the political battle in Whitehall. It was heartening to see all the Regiments of the Scottish Division pulling together.

The Army top brass did not perform with conviction. One of the saddest reflections of the campaign was the remark accredited to the Director of Infantry (of all people), along the lines of: "We could have achieved these 'add-backs' a lot quicker if it had not been for these damned protest movements." Who's kidding whom?

No campaign is fought without casualties, and the regiment owes a great debt of gratitude, not only to Donald, but to his wife, Pat, for putting up with as much separation as 1 KOSB, and to his brother, Jock, who continued to run the family business with one partner AWOL.

I commend this book most warmly to all Borderers and to a much wider public who hold the Scottish Regiments in especial regard. It is a thrilling tale - with a happy ending.

CONTENTS

Operation Borderer could never have been the success it was without the outstanding support of the following:

Brigadier Colin Mattingley
Brigadier Allan Alstead
Brigadier Frank Coutts
Brigadier Bob Riddle
Colonel Mike Ashmore (Royal Scots)
Major William Turner (Operation Borderer West)
Col Colin Hogg (KOSB Regimental Secretary) and his staff
The Committee of Keep Our Scottish Battalions led by
Lt Gen Sir John MacMillan
Graham Thomson
Michael Hall (photographer)
Pipe Major David Bunyan
Pipe Major David Sanderson
Charlie Laidlaw (Scottish & Westminster Communications)
Borders Regional Council
Ettrick & Lauderdale District Council
Roxburgh District Council
Berwickshire District Council
The Mayor of Berwick and the Border Provosts
Sir Hector Munro MP
Ian Lang MP
Sir David Steel MP
John Home-Robertson MP
Archie Kirkwood MP
Douglas Robson (Friends of the Gordon Highlanders)
and the many thousands of ex-Borderers who supported our rallies and
wrote letters to Government

Financial contributors to Operation Borderer

R & P Adam Ltd
Craigvaar Construction Ltd
Crawford Builders Ltd
H Cartwright Esq
J Cockburn (Butcher)
Edinburgh Woollen Mill Ltd
John Gaskell Esq, Connecticut, USA
Murray and Burrell Ltd
Macqueen Printers Ltd
Meigle Printers Ltd
William Lockie Ltd
W S Robertson Ltd
Royal British Legion Galashiels Club
Royal British Legion Kelso Club
Royal British Legion Selkirk Club
The Border Public
Many members of the Regiment

Chapter 1

A Short History of
The King's Own Scottish Borderers

For many centuries the men of the Borders have been celebrated as hardy and courageous fighters. The fame of the "reivers" or raiders, who used to penetrate deep into England, has been immortalised in the old ballads, which are known all over the world. These record the doings of Scotts and Armstrongs, Kers and Elliots, Johnstones and Jardines, and other famous Border names. In those days the Border clans fought usually only for themselves and the valleys in which they lived; only when Scotland as a whole was threatened would they band together. Sir Walter Scott had this in mind when he wrote of Ettrick and Teviotdale, Eskdale and Liddesdale, in the famous song which has become the Regimental March: for in time of national danger the men of these valleys would cease to think and to fight simply for their own valley, they would join forces for Scotland: "A' the Blue Bonnets are Bound for the Border".

As time went on, our loyalties became wider, and while each family remained as proud as ever of its reputation of its own valley, and as determined as ever that it should outshine its neighbours in the virtues of hardiness and courage, the Borderers came to look upon themselves as the keepers of the gates of Scotland. As loyalties became wider still, they offered their services of hand and heart to Britain as a whole, though they still remained Scottish, still Borderers, and still proud to uphold the reputation of their own particular valley and family.

One November day in 1688 - it was Guy Fawkes' Day as it happens - King William III landed in the south of England from Holland, and the reigning Stuart King, James II and VII, fled the country within a month. Powerful interests in Scotland were bent on restoring King James to his throne, and a Stuart Army under Graham of Claverhouse ("Bonnie Dundee") began forming in the Highlands. In March 1689, David Leslie, 3rd Earl of Leven, who was both the son and the grandson of distinguished soldiers, and who had travelled to England with King William, was authorised to raise a Regiment of 800 men in Edinburgh "by beat of drum".

He got his men in two hours, parading them near St Giles's. One can imagine with what urgency they trained, for within four months they were marching out to their first battle. This was fought at Killiecrankie, near Pitlochry in Perthshire, on the 27th July; and although the rebel Highlanders had the best of the day, Lord Leven's Regiment held its ground until ordered to with-draw, which they did in splendid order. Bonnie Dundee was killed in the battle and the rebellion died out with his death; and as for the Regiment, the Lord Provost and magistrates of Edin-burgh were so proud of their showing in the field that they conferred on it the right to recruit for ever in Edinburgh without asking leave, and the right to march through the city with bayonets fixed and Colours flying.

That Regiment was destined in time to become renowned as The King's Own Scottish Borderers. No wonder that the Regi-mental ties with Edinburgh have remained so close ever since.

King James's cause was lost in Scotland, but not yet in Ireland; and thither the Regiment went, to fight several successful battles within a year. In 1691 it went for the first of many times to the continent of Europe to fight the French in Flanders. After four weary years of battle, it played a prominent part in the capture of Namur in 1695. Here the French were fighting with a new type

10

of bayonet, which could remain fixed while the musket was being fired; whereas the Regiment, like the rest of the British, were still using the old type, which had to be stuck into the muzzle. The French gained little from their advantage, for the Regiment, despite it, swept them off the field and carried their objective. "Namur, 1695" was a tough and stubborn fight, well worthy of its place at the head of our Battle Honours.

Some years later the regiment returned to Scotland, where there were still threats of trouble from those Highland Clans who remained faithful to the Stuarts. These threats developed into the Rebellion of 1715; and the Regiment, now known as "The 25th (Edinburgh) Regiment of Foot", took part in the Battle of Sheriffmuir, just north of Stirling. Like Killiecrankie, the battle itself was indecisive, but the result was fatal to the rebels.

In 1762 the Regiment began a long period of service abroad. Ten years in Gibraltar, a short spell in Ireland, three years in the West Indies: these were followed by two years in Flanders, culminating in the battle of Fontenoy in May 1745, where they suffered the loss of over 200 officers and men. In that year, once more and for the last time, the Stuart faction in Scotland raised a rebellion, the famous "Forty-Five", and the regiment returned in October to garrison Edinburgh Castle, and to take part in the Battle of Culloden, which put an end to the Stuart hopes for all time.

The Regiment's next battle was among the most famous ever fought by the British Army. The little town of Minden, in Germany, lies in the jaws of an important pass through a long, narrow, rugged range of hills; and this pass has been fought for by many armies since the dawn of history: even the ancient Romans fought there. On the 1st of August 1759, six Regiments of British Infantry, some 2,000 men all told, advanced alone against 10,000 crack French cavalry, and defeated them. The 25th (Edinburgh) Regiment of Foot was one of these British Regiments.

As the six Regiments advanced against the enemy, through the rose gardens of Minden town towards the narrow gap in the range that towered above them, they picked roses and stuck them in their bonnets; and in common with the other five Regiments that share the honour of Minden, The King's Own Scottish Borderers of today wear roses in their bonnets on Minden Day, the 1st August of every year.

In 1763 the war ended, the Regiment returned to Britain, and the Colours which they had carried for twenty years in many battles were buried with full Military Honours in St Nicholas's Church, Newcastle-on-Tyne. There followed five years at home; eight in Minorca; seven at home; ten in Gibraltar; long years of garrison duty and of keeping the peace. And then, in 1792, there came a new experience: for five years the Regiment was based in Plymouth, and served at sea in detachments on board various of His Majesty's Ships. It was a profitable form of duty, for officers and men alike shared in the prize money.

Two parties were lucky enough to be serving in Admiral Hood's squadron when it captured a Spanish prize with a million pounds on board: captains received £1,500 each, subalterns £900, and the men were so flush with money that, having been landed at Portsmouth and told to march back to Plymouth, they paid for the church bells to be rung for them in every town and village on the route. Three other detachments were serving under Lord Howe when he won the battle of the Glorious First of June.

After a short spell in the West Indies, the Regiment returned to Britain, and thence to a short campaign in Holland in 1799, where its third Battle Honour, of Egmont-op-Zee, was won. Here the Regiment carried out a brilliant operation as Advanced Guard; but the campaign as a whole was not a success, and the expedition was withdrawn to England, arriving on Halloween. Napolean had by now risen to command the French Armies, and was making a bold attempt to capture Egypt. The Regiment sailed in May 1801 to join the British Forces in that country, and found that the French has been dislodged from all of it except the city and port of Alexandria. The siege of Alexandria, and with it the French designs on Egypt, ended with the enemy's surrender on the 3rd September, and the Regiment returned once more to England. The part which it had played in these operations is commemorated with the symbol of the Sphinx, with the word EGYPT inscribed above it, which is borne to this day on our Colours.

In 1805, under the authority of King George III, the Regiment became known officially as "The King's Own Borderers", thus becoming a Royal Regiment, with the honour of wearing blue facings instead of yellow as hitherto. He commanded us also to carry the Royal Crest in the first and fourth corners of the Regimental Colour, with the Motto *In Veritate Religionis Confido* ("I put my Trust in the Truth of Religion"); and in the second and third corners the White Horse of Hanover, with the Motto *Nec Aspera Terrent* ("Let Not Hardships Deter Us"). Nothing could have been more appropriate than the White Horse of Hanover upon the Colours of a Regiment which had fought under its sovereigns for close on a century, and defended it twice against the Stuarts. The old motto of the City of Edinburgh, *Nisi Dominus Frustra*, was and still is retained: it means literally "Without the Lord All is in Vain", and the words are the beginning of the Latin version of the first verse of the 127th Psalm: "Except the Lord build the House, they labour in vain that build it". Not until 1887 did the present proud title, by which the Regiment is known all over the world of "The King's Own Scottish Borderers", become our official designation.

From 1807 to 1817 the Regiment served once again in the West Indies, and the next forty years were spread over England, the West Indies again, Ireland, South Africa, India, and (once more) Gibraltar. In 1859 a 2nd Battalion was raised. This, in fact, was the third time that such a thing had happened; but both the previous 2nd Battalions, raised respectively in 1795 and 1805,

13

had been short-lived. The Battalions raised in 1859 was more fortunate, and was to bring much honour to the Regiment until, in common with every other 2nd Battalion of the Line, it was disbanded in 1947 after the Second World War.

In 1881 a grievous threat developed against the Regiment: it was to lose its Scottish identity and be based upon York. York lies a good deal farther south than even the reivers of old were accustomed to penetrate; and after violent protests the Depot was established at Berwick-upon-Tweed, where it remains to this day. In 1888 the 2nd Battalion fought its first action in Egypt; in 1889 the 1st Battalion fought in Burma; and in 1895 the 2nd Battalion took part in the Chitral Relief Expedition, one of the classic operations in the history of the North-West Frontier of India. Two years later it formed part of the no less famous Tirah Expedition, and fought twenty-three gruelling little actions among icy hills, in chilling winds, and on short rations.

In 1898 there was a change in the Regiment's Dress. In 1882 it has been authorised to wear tartan; and in common with all other Scots Regiments who had not received a special dispensation to do otherwise, it had donned the so-called "universal" or "Government" tartan, originally designed for the Black Watch and worn by that Regiment to this day. In 1898, after prolonged efforts by the Regiment, strongly supported by the then Earl of Leven and Melville (the Head of the House of Leslie), permission was given for the Leslie tartan to be worn instead. Thus, two hundred and nine years after the 3rd Earl had raised his gallant eight hundred men in the close of St Giles's in Edinburgh, and in the lifetime of the 11th Earl, the Regiment was able to assume the tartan of its first Colonel. The Pipers continued to wear, as they still do, the tartan of the Royal Stuarts; this they have done since the early eighteen-hundreds, presumably with the permission of the Stuarts' Hanoverian successor. There is no record of such permission being granted originally, and final written approval for the wearing of this tartan was only given in 1920.

The 1st Battalion took part in the South African War, winning the further Battle Honours of "Paardeberg" and "South Africa, 1900-1902". In South Africa also was won its first Victoria Cross, when Lieut Coulson was awarded it for gallantry at Lambrecht Fontein.

With the outbreak of the First World War we come down to modern times. The 1st Battalion was in India and the 2nd in Ireland. The 2nd was among the first units to come to grips with the enemy, playing a heroic part in the Retreat from Mons in 1914, including the desperate battle of Le Cateau, and in the so-called Battle of Marne and on the Aisne. In the hard fighting around La Bassee and Neuve Chapelle it played a leading part, and other Battalions, newly raised for the War, went out to France as 1915 wore on. In September 1915, at the Battle of Loos, Piper Daniel Laidlaw of the 7th Battalion won one of the most famous Victoria Crosses of all time, for playing his pipes up and down the parapet of a trench during a critical moment of the fight. The Regiment was represented at the Somme in 1916, at Arras and Vimy Ridge in 1917, and in the desperate fight in the Spring of 1918. Three other Victoria Crosses were won, one in the 5th Battalion and two in the 1st.

The 1st Battalion, for all that it had been in India on the outbreak of war, was not long behind the 2nd in getting into action. Once again they were to arrive in time to take part in a battle destined to be famous in history, for they were among the troops to land on "Y" Beach in Gallipoli, at dawn on Sunday the 25th of April 1915. Other landings met with greater success, and the "Y" Beach operation was abandoned after thirty-four hours ashore, during which 296 officers and men were killed and wounded; nine officers, including the Commanding Officer, were among the killed. The 4th and 5th Battalions also fought in Gallipoli, and later in Palestine, before going, like the 1st, to Flanders.

Between the wars, the two Regular Battalions took their share of duties at home and abroad, while the 4th and 5th (Territorial) Battalions grew their roots once more in the countryside of southern Scotland. Two notable landmarks in the history of the Regiment belong to the years immediately before the Second World War. The first was the appointment of Her Royal Highness, The Duchess of Gloucester, herself a Scott of Buccleuch, as the first Colonel-in-Chief of The King's Own Scottish Borderers. The second was a remarkable parade in 1939, to commemorate the 250th anniversary of the raising of the Regiment. The 2nd Battalion was abroad; but the 1st, 4th, 5th, 6th and 7th were all represented on parade. Led by the massed Pipe Bands, and exercising their privilege of marching with bayonets fixed and Colours flying, they marched from near Holyrood House to the Mound, where Her Royal Highness, supported by the 13th Earl of Leven and Melville, took the salute. Thirty-seven days later, Britain was at war again.

The 1st Battalion was early on the Continent, and fought its way stubbornly back to Dunkirk; it landed in Normandy in 1944, and amply revenged itself before reaching Hamburg about VE Day. The 2nd Battalion fought for three years in Burma. The 4th and 5th Battalions were in the 52nd Lowland Division, which, trained as mountain troops, finally landed in the Island of Walcheren, and fought below sea level. The 6th Battalion shared the fortunes of the 15th Scottish Division, fighting across three countries into Germany. The 7th Battalion was dropped at Arnhem, and suffered its full share of the heavy casualties sustained there.

1947 saw the disappearance of the 2nd Battalion, whose splendid tradition and history are now merged in those of the 1st after eighty-eight years of parallel existence. In April 1951 the 1st Battalion sailed for Korea, destined for hard fighting against the Communist forces. The month of October showed increasing activity, and on the 4th of November the enemy put in a ferocious attack, heralded by a bombardment at the rate of a hundred shells a minute. The Battle went on all night against an enemy who was reckoned to outnumber the defenders by ten to one. The Battalion held its ground, and Private William Speakman won the Victoria Cross.

In recent years the Regiment have served with distinction in Malaya, Berlin, Belize and Northern Ireland.

When the 3rd Earl of Leven raised his Regiment in Edinburgh "by beat of drum" on a March day in 1689, he did so in the face of an emergency, and to meet a crisis. He was confident of getting his men, and he got them in two hours. One wonders whether he ever dreamed that he was raising, not eight hundred men for an emergency which would be dissipated in a few weeks' time, but a Regiment which would endure for centuries. Those drum-beats in the shadow of St Giles's have echoed in corners of the world which were undreamed of in Lord Leven's day.

Chapter 2

Introduction to the Main Participants
in Operation Borderer

A brief introductory sketch of the main participants:

ALSTEAD FAL CBE Brigadier, (Retired) KOSB,
  Chief Executive Scottish Sports Council. Former Officer
  Commanding Highland Division.
ASHMORE M OBE Colonel, (Retired) The Royal Scots,
  Former Staff Officer, Ministry of Defence.
BRUCE Ian,
  Defence Correspondent, *The Herald.*
CAMPBELL JCF Major, (Retired) Black Watch,
  The man who started it all.
CARRELL Severin,
  Defence Correspondent, *The Scotsman.*
CHRISTY Campbell,
  Defence correspondent, *The Daily Telegraph.*
COUTTS FH CBE DL Brigadier, (Retired) KOSB,
  Former Colonel KOSB. Former Scottish Internationalist and
  President of the SRU. Author of *One Blue Bonnet.*
FRASER K Major,
  Assistant Regimental Secretary.
GOMME DUNCAN M Major, (Retired) Black Watch,
  A faithful and regular supporter.

GRAHAM Campbell Major, (Retired) Scots Guards,
   The voice of Edinburgh.
HALL M,
   Regimental Historian. Photographer (responsible for photo-
   graphs in this book).
HAMILTON A The Rt Hon MP,
   Minister of State for the Armed Forces under Rt Hon T. King.
HOGG CG Lt Colonel, (Retired),
   Regimental Secretary The KOSB.
INGE General Sir Peter KCB,
   Chief of the General Staff.
KEEL Paul,
   Defence Correspondent, *Mail on Sunday*.
KING T The Rt Hon MP,
   The Secretary of State for Defence until April 1992.
LAIDLAW C,
   Director Citigate Scotland Ltd. Organiser/spokesman Keep
   Our Scottish Battalions Committee. A master of delegation.
LANG I The Rt Hon MP,
   Secretary of State for Scotland.
LEVEY J Brigadier, (Retired),
   Chairman Save our Staffords Campaign.
LYALL J Drum Major, (Retired),
   Former Senior Drum Major of the Scottish Division.
MACMILLAN Sir J Lt General KCB, CBE (Retired),
   Argyll and Sutherland Highlanders. Chairman "Keep Our
   Scottish Battalions" Committee. Scotland owes him a great
   debt.
MATTINGLEY CG CBE Brigadier, (Retired),
   Colonel The King's Own Scottish Borderers.
MINTO The Rt Hon Earl of OBE JP,
   Convenor Borders Regional Council.

NAYYAR Simon,
   Lobbyist, Westminster Communications.
RIFKIND M The Rt Hon MP,
   The Secretary of State for Defence from April 1992.
ROBSON D, Royal Navy (Retired),
   Press Secretary - 'Friends of the Gordon Highlanders' - phone
   number on application to MoD or Cheltenham Listening
   Post.
ROBSON MM Captain, (Retired),
   Chairman 'Friends of the Gordon Highlanders'.
RIDDLE RW OBE Brigadier, (Retired),
   British Legion Scotland.
SANDERSON R Lord,
   Chairman Conservative Party (Ex-Borderer).
SWANSTON J, 7th Battalions KOSB,
   Re-Union Secretary. Peebleshire co-ordinator - Operation
   Borderer.
THOMSON CG MM,
   6th Battalion KOSB Re-Union Secretary. Office Manager,
   Operation Borderer.
TURNER W Major, MC (Retired),
   Co-ordinator Operation Borderer (West). A powerful force.
WALKER L Mrs,
   Mother of Stewart, Lt Colonel, KOSB Whipper-in.

Chapter 3

Options for Change

On the 23rd July 1991, The Secretary of State for Defence announced that, as part of "Options for Change," The Royal Scots and The King's Own Scottish Borderers were to be amalgamated. This amalgamation coupled to the amalgamation of The Queen's Own Highlanders and The Gordon Highlanders, and the loss of the 2nd Battalion The Scots Guards made the impact of the overall cuts from 55 Infantry Battalions to 38 disproportionately severe to the Scottish Division, especially as 3 Royal Marine Commando Battalions were also to be retained.

Brigadier FAL Alstead CBE was asked by the Colonel of the Regiment Brigadier CG Mattingley CBE, to take charge of Operation Borderer. He did much to initiate the Campaign, but later had to adopt a low profile because of his job as Chief Executive of the Scottish Sports Council, answerable to the Secretary of State for Scotland. He remained a tower of strength behind the scenes during the Campaign, and his duties were assumed by Brigadier FH Coutts CBE. Many King's Own Scottish Borderer Officers and men made huge contributions to the Campaign by exerting pressure on government, but some due to political and business constraints must remain anonymous. In telling the story of Operation Borderer I respect their position. No report on the operation would be complete without acknowledgement of the contribution made by our Colonel Colin

Mattingley, and of our local Members of Parliament, The Rt Hon Sir Hector Monro MP, The Rt Hon Sir David Steel MP, John Home-Robertson MP, and Archie Kirkwood MP.

Chapter 4

Setting up the Campaign

I first met Allan Alstead when I joined the 1st Battalion of Kings Own Scottish Borderers at Selerang Barracks in Singapore in 1957. Allan was a career Soldier acting as Signals Officer, and I was a somewhat reluctant National Service Subaltern deployed in C Company. Little did we know how our paths were to cross some 34 years later, although we had kept in touch as I had introduced Allan to his wife Joy at a memorable barbecue at Cauldshiels Loch in the Heart of the Borders. The only reason I had been sent up for Officer selection was that I had been a member of the Army Cadet Force whilst at school at Gordonstoun in Morayshire. The school Cadet Force were attached to the Seaforth Highlanders, and our camps were always held at Fort George near Inverness. We were always reluctant to go to camp, as it was held during the first two weeks of our summer holiday, and we had to wash our dishes in a filthy communal tank outside the cookhouse, which was always covered by a film of grease and particles of tinned tomato and beans, greatly favoured by Army cooks. In addition we had to wear the horribly prickly uniform, normally only worn once a week at school, for two whole weeks. The housemaster who commanded the school Army Cadet Force was Major Downton whose claim to fame was that he could assemble a bren-gun in the dark. We were not surprised by this, as he was almost totally blind. He taught scripture in school, and

I never understood how he equated his dual role.

Having passed my part one and two in the Cadets I attained the heady heights of an OR.1. I was sent to the War Office selection board and given a "deferred watch", largely because I destroyed the thinking behind one of their tasks. I was required to transport two barrels between two poles with the use of a rope, and the help of six other potential leaders, all full of good ideas, without touching the intervening ground. I managed to get all the men and the barrels across and found myself remaining; without the use of the rope which had fallen into no man's land. I completely mucked up the exercise by jumping some 20 feet to complete the task. The Officer in charge said it was impossible, which I found strange as I had just done it. The Army thinking was that some fluke had occurred. They did not know that I was Border High Jump (no. 2 in Scotland), Long Jump and Triple Jump champion. I spent three months at Berwick as a Lance Corporal before returning to beat their assault course again. I was sent for to hear the result of my two days of hell, to be told by the Commanding Officer, "you have buggered up our assault course twice, and although we do not think you make enough of yourself, we are going to pass you. Do you have any preference for regiments, you can have three choices?" I replied, "KOSB, KOSB, KOSB." My friend Mike Cook, who played scrum half for both Gala and Selkirk, and who borrowed my cavalry twill trousers, razor blades, and toothpaste at Eaton Hall was sent to the Royal Scots as he gave them as a second choice. I was sure it was because he wanted to avoid returning my trousers.

Also serving at Selerang was Major Frank Coutts, at that time a Company Commander who, like Allan, was to attain the rank of Brigadier. I was to meet Frank, an adopted son of Melrose, often, after leaving the Army, in his capacity as a member of the SRU and ultimately as President of the Union. Frank was also to figure prominently in the Campaign to save the Regiment.

Frank had done much in his time as Colonel of the Regiment

24

to humanise the position of Colonel and is greatly admired by all sections of the Regiment. His devilish sense of humour and dislike of humbug made him a powerful force in uniting all Borderers in the initial stages of the Campaign.

After Defence Secretary Tom King's announcement of "Options for Change" in July 1991, it was decided at senior level within the Regiment that we would fight the proposal to amalgamate the Borderers with the Royal Scots with all means at our disposal, so that when my telephone rang on 7th August and Allan Alstead asked me to co-ordinate Operation Borderer in the east, much had already been done, including the formation of the Keep Our Scottish Battalions committee, embracing all the regiments in the Scottish Division under the leadership of General Sir John MacMillan, a former GOC Scotland. On the 10th August Regimental Headquarters issued the following press release. . .

FROM RHQ KOSB BERWICK UPON TWEED

PRESS RELEASE
(Embargoed to 1000 hrs on 10th August 1991)

"Back the Borderers - Save the KOSB" - this is the battle-cry of Operation Borderer which is the Campaign to save The King's Own Scottish Borderers from amalgamation. The Campaign is to be launched in Edinburgh on Saturday 10 August - by a trio of KOSB Brigadiers: Frank Coutts, Bob Riddle and Allan Alstead of the Borderers' Association.

The Campaign reflects the enormous resentment which has been created in Scotland by the way the Scottish regiments have been treated in the government's cuts. Why is it, for instance, that 6 Scottish regiments are to be lost, while in the whole of England only 4 are to go?

No-one in commerce would think of shedding effective parts of a company during a reorganisation - the loss making bad performing elements are the ones removed. What the government is doing here to

25

our well recruited and highly effective Scottish regiments flies in the face of both commercial and military logic. The country will be left with insufficient Battalions of Infantry to meet our military commitments.

Operation Borderer will co-ordinate the voices of the supporters of the KOSB and will ensure that the strongest message is delivered to Ministers and MPs, loud and clear! The Operation will complement similar work of other Regimental Associations throughout Scotland.

The government can expect a hard fought Campaign now that the gloves have been removed. All soldiers in Scotland, both serving and retired, as well as many thousands of their families, friends and supporters, are very angry indeed. They have but one aim - to secure an add-back by the government of at least one Battalion which will remove the need to amalgamate.

A Press Conference will be held at the Officers' Mess, Redford Barracks, Colinton, Edinburgh, EH13 0PP, at 1000 hrs on Saturday, 10th August 1991. Photograph and TV opportunities will be available.

Contacts Lt Col David Ward
Regimental Headquarters KOSB
The Barracks
Berwick upon Tweed TD15 1DG
Tel: (0289) 307426/7 Fax: (0289) 331928

Brigadier Allan Alstead
Tel: (Office) 031 317 7200 (7201 after 1700 hrs)
(Home) 031 556 5599

On 14th August a meeting took place at Whitefoord House in Edinburgh, the subject . . . a meeting of the Scottish Generals Committee "Keep Our Scottish Battalions". In attendance were General Sir John MacMillan (Chair), General Sir David Young, General Sandy Boswell, representatives from all seven Scottish regiments, Colin Campbell's group, and representatives from Citigate Scotland Ltd, a public relations firm who were retained to organise the Campaign. Colin Campbell was the man who initiated the Campaign as soon as "Options for Change" was announced. He called a meeting in Perth of other activists at which "Keep our Scottish Battalions" was born. Two full time Secretaries were appointed - Colonel Hamish Logan and Colonel Ian Cameron. Charlie Laidlaw of Citigate was appointed Campaign Organiser responsible to General Sir John MacMillan the Campaign Chairman. The meeting decided on a petition to Parliament organised nationally, and petition forms were to be in place in each Regimental area by 19th August. Scotland had decided to fight.

Meanwhile in the heart of the Regimental area in Galashiels a meeting of Borderers was called which included all the Border Provosts and was attended by Allan Alstead and Frank Coutts. The Provosts were unanimous in their support, saying "give us a fact sheet on one sheet of paper so we know what to say in backing the regiment". This fact sheet was quickly put together and is reproduced below.

KEEP OUR SCOTTISH BATTALIONS

The Facts

• The Secretary of State for Defence has proposed to Parliament that the Infantry is to be reduced from 55 to 38 battalions with, additionally, 3 Royal Marine Commando battalions. This is insufficient to carry out the tasks set out in the document 'Britain's Army for the '90s' (published by HMSO in July 1991).

• The impact of the cuts on Scotland is disproportionately severe.

• No credit is given for the proven ability of Scotland to man Her Battalions when other parts of the country have shown that they cannot sustain their local regiments. Likewise no credit has been given to the quality of our soldiers nor their cost effectiveness.

• Reductions in the size of the Scottish Infantry will cause the loss of 1800 jobs in the long term. Such a scale of redundancies will not apply in any other part of the country, since the battalions to be cut will not be at full strength. These job losses come on top of recent losses in the steel and mining industries.

• The impact of the amalgamations breaches one principle previously advanced by the Chief of the General Staff by affecting a regiment which has already been amalgamated since the War - The Queen's Own Highlanders - and also marks the end of the unbroken existence of the senior British Regiment of the Line, and arguably the oldest in the world - The Royal Scots.

The Campaign

The campaign's aim is to persuade the government that the cuts it proposes are too severe to be justified, and to ensure that Scotland's case for retaining its Battalions is recognised.

With Your Help We Will Win!

What You Can Do

• Sign the petition. Signatures are being gathered all over Scotland.
• If you can, please donate to the campaign funds.
• If you want to help in the campaign, please write to Campaign Headquarters or telephone our hotline 0898 234 232.
• ABOVE ALL please write to your MP.

WITH YOUR HELP WE CAN WIN THIS CAMPAIGN AND KEEP OUR SCOTTISH BATTALIONS

At this stage it was difficult to get over to the public that serving Officers and Soldiers could not take part in the Campaign because of the nature of their terms of employment. It was up to the "Old and Bold" to demonstrate, write letters and march at Rallies. Operation Borderer's task was to solicit support from all sections of the public, and the media. This we set about doing.

Soon after Tom King's announcement of "Options for Change," I had been approached by an old friend Graham Thomson who had served with great distinction in the 6th Battalion KOSB during the War, and who had won the Military Medal with the Battalion. Graham, known as "Ginger" to his friends was known as an enthusiastic hard working member of the Regimental family, having run the 6th Battalion Reunion Club since the War. Graham had the reputation of working on a short fuse, and during the Campaign we had many amusing incidents, and sometimes brushes with senior members of the Campaign.

Graham and I decided that we needed a town centre base for the collection of signatures on the petition, and soon found a vacant shop in Market Street, Galashiels which we opened on 21st August as a public office. We obtained drums, and Regimental tartan, from RHQ to dress the windows and organised a rota of volunteers to man the shop.

The shop was opened by Drum Major Jock Lyall (Rtd) to the skirl of the pipes before a large gathering of ex-Borderers and television news cameras at the exact moment the petition was being launched by Moira Anderson on Calton Hill in Edinburgh in 21st August, 1991. The first day the office was open we obtained 3000 signatures on the petition, and had countless visits from people handing in Regimental memorabilia for the office, which soon became a mini museum. By twisting a few arms we obtained a telephone line within 24 hours which proved invaluable in co-ordinating the Campaign.

By now my counterpart in the west, Major Willie Turner, MC, has been appointed, and assisted by Major Alec Grieve, they were up and running and already had a letter out to all known supporters, which is reproduced here. . .

Dumfries 16th August, 1991

Dear Borderer,

I have been tasked with co-ordinating the local Campaign to Back the Borderers and am seeking help to set up a network of support throughout Dumfries and Galloway.

I am sharing the responsibility of this task with Major William Turner MC whom you may have already heard on local radio and seen in the Press. His renowned enthusiasm and commitment will be useful, but *your* help is essential.

The Regimental plan is to attack the government decision with every means at our disposal in order to reverse it, but it must be made clear at the outset that any adverse comment towards other Scottish regiments is wasteful and fundamentally detrimental to the Campaign.

The attack is to consist of three main thrusts:

1) At Individuals - Government Ministers and MPs of all parties both local and national. Weapons - Multitudinous individual letters based on briefing notes (to follow).

2) At Institutions - Parliament, Regional and District Councils and any other suitable organisation. Weapons - Individual letters and lobbying at every opportunity. Press and TV coverage.

3) At the general public. Weapons - Barrages of posters and stickers. Public petition. A well-orchestrated Campaign with a high media profile. Rallies and marches.

A great deal of work has been done behind the scenes and is continuing, but a properly orchestrated Campaign is soon to be launched which will involve national and local media (TV, radio and newspapers), a formal petition aiming for maximum signatures, a poster and car sticker campaign and mass rallies/marches.

We are communicating on a daily basis with Brigadier Alstead in

Edinburgh, who is Chairman of the Regimental Campaign Committee. We are also in direct contact with RHQ and the co-ordinators of the Campaign in the Eastern Borders.

As you might expect, the Royal Scots are also shocked at this harsh decision and are fighting hard. They are our allies in this battle and have the advantage of working from the relatively tight perimeter of their recruiting area. As always, we have to cover a much larger area, including Lanarkshire.

Therefore, we need to set up small committees in each centre of population from Langholm to Portpatrick with direct communications with us in Dumfries so that necessary information can be passed quickly to every supporter in the Region.

THIS IS WHERE YOU COME IN

1) GET IN TOUCH NOW with as many ex-Borderers and other likely supporters as possible in your local area and start compiling lists of names, addresses and telephone numbers.

2) APPOINT from your number AN ORGANISER/SPOKESMAN and transmit his name, address and telephone number to us. A 24 hr ansaphone service is at Dumfries (0387) 59989. More urgent messages may be left at my office at 37 Castle Street, Dumfries (0387 54424).

3) KEEP LOOKING for more supporters for this important cause. The minimum requirement is only to fill a page of signatures for the petition.

For our part, we will be pressing for the Campaign literature for distribution to the local committees. For this purpose we need DISTRIBUTION/COLLECTION points in Langholm, Lockerbie, Moffat, Thornhill, Sanquhar/Kirkconnel, Kirkcudbright, New Galloway/Dalry, Newton Stewart, Wigtown and Stranraer. My firm has agreed to allow our offices in Dumfries, Castle Douglas and Annan to be used for this purpose.

We will also require as many people as possible to write to their MP and Councillors but we will be circulating advice notes of the relevant facts to assist.

31

Ultimately, the success of this operation depends upon the strength and spread of support throughout the region. We have to get weaving to ensure that the maximum amount of publicity is achieved before the Defence debate at the beginning of October when Parliament re-convenes.

Don't think that it is too late in the day to mount a useful Campaign or that it is a hopeless cause. With your support, we can achieve a great deal by a short and voluble effort from all quarters - we have nothing to lose and much to gain.

If this is to be the Regiment's last battle after 302 valiant years, we owe it to our forebears to make it a really bloody one.

WE WILL WIN

Major A G Grieve TD Regional Co-ordinator

ONCE A BORDERER - ALWAYS A BORDERER.

STOP PRESS

1. The national "Keep Our Scottish Battalions" Campaign is being launched to TV and press with Moira Anderson as VIP at 10.30 hrs Wednesday 21st August on Calton Hill, Edinburgh (east end of Princes Street). Maximum attendance required, including wives, children, cousins and aunts. Wear medals. Whip up anyone who can go. It may be too late to organise bus transport but have a day in Edinburgh and you can always enjoy the Festival afterwards.

2. The Campaign is being professionally orchestrated by Citigate, a PR firm whose successes include the War Widows Pensions. Citigate will be producing a Fact Sheet for distribution.

3. Petition forms will soon be on hand for distribution and filling. Any forms already used are OK. Deadline for delivery to collection points MONDAY 30TH SEPTEMBER.

When Allan Alstead asked me early in August to organise Operation Borderer East, I made a decision to resign not only from the local Conservative Club where I was a committee member, but from the Conservative Party. I felt it was not possible to conduct a vigorous anti-government campaign and remain a member of that Party. Most members of the Party locally understood my position, but there was some resentment from a small number of people, who even refused to sign the petition.

My only real contribution to the local Party had been some years previously when I had agreed to put up the Prospective Parliamentary Candidate, at the time one Stuart Thom, for the weekend. We had a Myna Bird with quite an amazing vocabulary which I purchased from a local newsagent of doubtful background, although his brother is an ex-Borderer. We invited some people in, (the list was given to me by the local agent) and during the evening Stuart Thom was telling us how he was going to win the seat. The Bird who had been sitting with his head cocked, listening attentively, suddenly interjected "Ho Ho you must be joking." He then followed up with several bars of "The Sound of Music". We eventually had to get rid of the Bird, which had become an embarrassment, having accused the postman of being "a lay-about" and inviting the dustman to "come in and take a seat".

The Tweedale Ettrick and Lauderdale Prospective Parliamentary Candidate at this time was Lloyd Beat who did make efforts on our behalf by writing to government and the press, no doubt with an eye on the forthcoming General Election. His letter to Defence Secretary Tom King is reproduced here.

33

Tweedale, Ettrick & Lauderdale
Conservative & Unionist Association
68 Galapark
Galashiels
TD1 1EZ

12th August, 1991

Dear Mr King,

THE KINGS OWN SCOTTISH BORDERERS

I write concerning the recent decision to recommend the amalgamation of the King's Own Scottish Borderers and the Royal Scots. As you will no doubt appreciate this has caused upset and fury among many people in this area. It also appears difficult to defend the decision on the grounds of maintaining an effective Army to meet the country's continuing defence needs. The KOSB has an excellent recruitment record and well over three hundred years of effective and loyal service in defending this nation.

Like many, if not all, Conservatives, I welcome the opportunity we have to reap a "peace Dividend". Furthermore there is no doubt that the standing Army must be reduced in size. It would offend against the principles of prudent Conservative administration if we were to fail to take the necessary tough decisions to reduce unnecessary expenditure and to provide the Army we need for the future. However, the effective termination of over three hundred years of effective KOSB service is an utterly incredible way to go about this matter.

The KOSB has a very effective recruitment record and finds no difficulty in keeping up to strength. It would appear that other regiments in England with far less successful records of recruitment are to continue in existence. Why? This hardly appears to be the way to build an effective Army.

If the Army is to be smaller, and some do suggest current plans will lead to the Army being too small, then the ability to increase recruitment quickly in times of need will become even more important. Evidence would suggest that the KOSB will be more than able to do this while some other, more modern, English regiments will have great difficulty.

Many of the regiments that are to be unaffected by the present defence review have very short histories. Others have been involved in amalgamation in recent times. Changes to these regiments would not wipe out hundreds of years of tradition and service. Once destroyed, it is impossible to recreate the continuity and tradition that means so much to the fighting man when called upon to serve his Nation.

Finally, I ask you to bear in mind the world renowned reputation of the Scottish Soldier. A reputation that stretches back for many hundreds of years. Why not play to these strengths in creating a modern defence establishment? The Scots have always played a more important role in our defence forces than the size of our population would suggest. To wipe away that history and close off this resource simply to satisfy a 1991 defence review would be shortsighted, potentially very dangerous for the United Kingdom and unjust.

I do wish you well in re-organising our defence forces to meet the challenges of the modern world. To deny our nation the services of the KOSB will not help in this process. I urge you to think again.

Yours sincerely

Lloyd Beat PPC

cc All Scottish Conservative MPs
Lord Sanderson of Bowden
Brigadier Allan Alstead CBE

By now the office in Market Street had become a hive of activity and our team of helpers were working well on a rota system. There were always two helpers in the office and one acting as a "whipper in" on the pavement, urging passers by to sign the petition. We also had teams out in Edinburgh, and at various Border events collecting signatures. In this nobody was more successful than Michael Hall, who stood in Edinburgh on the

Castle Esplanade for countless hours collecting signatures. Michael is a life long KOSB enthusiast, and a respected Regimental historian who has a magnificent collection of Regimental Cap Badges and artifacts. It was estimated that he personally collected 10,000 signatures on the petition, including a Russian and several Lithuanians, out of the total Border signatures numbering 108,000 sent to Edinburgh on the 1st October. Other helpers who made an outstanding contribution to the total were Mrs Lorraine Walker, mother of Lt Colonel Stewart Walker, who acted as "Chief Whipper In", and the redoubtable Jimmy Swanston from Peebles, a regular visitor to the office. One evening while buying an evening paper I overheard one Galashiels lady saying to another "Dinnae gang roond there, that wummuns there again", this was referring to Lorraine doing her act on the pavement.

In Dumfries and the West, Willie Turner was steadily collecting petition forms with the help of his team, and Sir Hector Monro was out helping on more than one occasion. This enabled the west to contribute 36,000 to our total of 108,000.

Early in September, Graham Thomson and I travelled to Hawick for a meeting organised by John Aitkin in the Ex-Service Club. We were anxious to try and establish an office in Hawick for the collection of signatures. The meeting was very well attended and chaired by John Aitkin, who served as an Officer with the 1st Battalion during National Service. By the time we left the meeting an office had been organised within the Town Hall and a rota for manning it drawn up.

By now we had established a "mini office" in Melrose within Adam Crawford's Art Shop and Gallery. Adam was distributing car stickers, posters and had petition forms for signing. Adam, better known locally as "Yid," had played in the second row with Frank Coutts for the Regiment and Melrose, and was a devout Borderer. He had originally been a builder, but had fallen out with his brother Jim over a wall which they had started at opposite ends and did not quite meet in the middle. Adam was a great help in publicising our Campaign.

We had also intimated that we had decided to hold a Rally in Galashiels on Saturday 21st September, and that a meeting of all Border Provosts and Council Convenors had been arranged for Tuesday 10th September at which the Regiment would provide a buffet lunch. Businesses and individuals who contributed to our funds were many and varied, and donations ranged from £5 from a Regimental widow to several thousand pounds from a local manufacturer. We solicited funds from as far away as Sydney in Australia, and the United States of America. We received one handsome dollar cheque from New York, which I gave to Graham Thomson our treasurer to pay into our bank in Galashiels. He went to the bank on rather a busy Friday morning to pay the cheque into Operation Borderer's account, to be told the Bank would have to charge £5 for so doing. A long and heated debate then took place in front of a large gathering in the bank, who were on a hiding to nothing as they had refused to display our Rally posters. Graham emerged from the bank unsuccessful and unrepentant, having told the management what he thought of them, to loud applause from the assembled customers.

The day following the Hawick meeting, Geoffrey Adam, Chairman of R & P Adam Chemical Manufacturers, telephoned and asked us to attend a meeting at his office in Selkirk. This was in response to a letter we had sent out to prominent businesses in the area asking for financial help. Seventy percent of the letters were answered enclosing a cheque for the fighting fund. Colonel Willie Bruce, Graham Thomson and myself attended the meeting with Geoff Adam, at which he told us of his plans to finance a record featuring a campaign tune on the A side and a Regimental tune called *Highland Cathedral* on the B side. This was to be handled by Citigate and recorded by the Murray International Whitburn Band and the Shotts and Dykehead Pipe Band. The record was to be produced by REL Studios and the sleeve designed by Hamilton Design, Edinburgh. In addition to this generous sponsorship we were to come away with a handsome cheque made out to Operation Borderer. The campaign tune entitled *Theme in Glory* composed by Alan Moorhouse was subsequently recorded along with *Highland Cathedral* composed by Michael Korb, and the record was launched at the studios of REL in Edinburgh after some very intensive recording sessions with Geoff Kingston who arranged the music. Due to distribution problems the record never achieved the success it deserved, but still remains a very good recording, and served the purpose of getting even wider coverage of the Campaign in the media. Geoffrey Adam has remained a staunch supporter of Keep Our Scottish Battalions throughout the Campaign.

I was instrumental in introducing Geoffrey to racing, now his main relaxation, (if racing can ever be relaxing) from his tremendous work-rate. Ken Oliver had asked me to organise a dinner party so he could meet Geoff, and this was arranged. Ken and Geoff got on like a house on fire, and after a very liquid dinner it transpired Geoff had agreed to buy a horse from Ken which he owned in partnership with Alan McTaggart. Ken had phoned Geoff the morning following the dinner party and said "you bought yourself one of the nicest young horses in Europe last night". Some days later an envelope was handed to me by Ken who said, "Well done . . . some commission for you". The envelope contained £300 in cash. When I next met Alan McTaggart, I told him there had been no need for commission as we had had a great party, to which he replied - "well, we thought £500 was about right!" I never did find out what Geoff paid for the horse which ended up being trained by me and winning at Kelso at 20 to 1 when Geoff was out of the country on business.

Many other businesses contributed to Operation Borderer, in particular McQueen Printers whose Managing Director, Michael Gray, is the son of a well known KOSB, the late Jimmy Gray who only ever wore one tie - the KOSB Regimental tie. Jimmy would have turned in his grave at the thought of Tom King's amalgamation proposals.

The meeting on 10th September of the Border Provosts, The Mayor of Berwick, and the Council Convenors took place in the Officers' Mess in Galashiels and was very well attended, with Officials of Regional and District Councils in the east and west, including the Rt Hon the Earl of Minto, OBE, JP, convenor of Borders Regional Council. Brigadier Allan Alstead CBE presided. There was 100% support for Operation Borderer and it was agreed that all present would do everything possible to help the Campaign. The subject of advertising for the Rally was discussed, as an advertisement in support of the Royal Scots had appeared in *The Scotsman* with the caption "supported by Local Government". I was asked to produce estimates of advertising costs for the Rally which were delivered by hand, some three hours after the conclusion of the meeting, at which we were assured the Councils would pay the costs of the advertisements. We were subsequently told that Local Government could not pay the costs, and having already placed the advertisements, we were left with £3000 advertising costs and £1200 in the bank. Fortunately members of the Regiment came to the rescue, although we were told that Edinburgh had provided finance for the Royal Scots advertisement. The day following the meeting the Earl of Minto wrote to Allan Alstead in the following terms. . .

Borders Regional Council Regional HQ
Newton St Boswells
Melrose
TD6 0SA

11 September 1991

Mr Dear Brigadier,

I left yesterday's meeting in Galashiels better informed than I had expected and, therefore, a relatively happy man. As I drove to Edinburgh I became less and less happy for I feel I failed in one important duty. In your concluding remarks you very kindly paid tribute to the actions of the Local Authorities. If I had not been searching in my mind for any points we might have overlooked, I should not, as the senior Borders Regional Councillor, have failed to have thanked you for your comments, for luncheon, for the briefing or to wish you every good fortune on behalf of my colleagues from both Regions and all Districts represented.

For this lapse I apologise and I take this opportunity to thank you - and through you - Brigadier Frank - for your hospitality and for putting us in the picture. You will have gathered, I trust, that you have the united support of every Council. If we are kept aware of the regiments needs we shall do our best to meet them where we are able.

Again my apologies for missing my cue yesterday.

With kind regards

Yours sincerely

Minto

Chapter 5

The Galashiels and Dumfries Rallies

A great deal of work had gone into the Galashiels Rally of 21st September in motivating the general public and ex-Borderers to attend, and also putting together a composite pipe band under Pipe Major David Bunyan of Selkirk. We had assembled a formidable platform party representing all political parties. Sir Nicholas Fairbairn QC MP, Sir David Steel MP, John Home-Robertson MP and Archie Kirkwood MP, supported by General Sir John MacMillan, Campaign Chairman, Brigadier Frank Coutts and Brigadier Colin Mattingley, the Colonel of the Regiment. The Rally was an outstanding success and was featured in the national television news on both channels. The press also gave wide coverage the following day and on the Monday. Some 700 ex-servicemen and women marched behind the Mass Bands to the Scott Park which was thronged with the public, to hear General Sir John MacMillan say "a country that skimps on defence, pays later in the lives of its' sons".

The Rally did much to unite Borderers in the fight due to the cross party presence on the platform. The cross party support was what was to cement public support and none of the speakers attempted to score political points. Sir Nicholas Fairbairn however could not resist telling us that Archie Kirkwood had been conceived in Trafalgar Square on VE day!

On Saturday the 28th September, Willie Turner organised a Rally in Dumfries. We were to form up at Whitesands at 3.20pm and march via the High Street to the Fountain. A bus was arranged from Galashiels picking up at Selkirk and Hawick, and some 30 ex-Borderers travelled to Dumfries. Unfortunately we were persuaded by the Hawick contingent to stop at Annan Ex-Service Club for refreshments, and by the time I persuaded them back on the bus we had a tight schedule to make the start of the Rally. In the event we had to disembark from the bus some way from the Whitesands and only four of us made the march, although all were present to hear Sir Hector Monro and Alec Shaw (Edinburgh KOSB Association) make an impassioned plea for the government to think again. We spent a pleasant afternoon and evening in the public houses in Dumfries and obtained many signatures on the petition. As at the Galashiels Rally, the event made the national television news.

The deadline for the return of petition forms was the 1st October, as they had to be counted, sorted and transported by train to London for handing over on the 14th October.

On Sunday the 6th October the Keep Our Scottish Battalions Committee organised a march from the Scottish Office to Waverley Station carrying the petition forms in boxes for delivery by train to London. General Sir John MacMillan supervised the loading of the petition boxes on to the London train, and was interviewed by press and television. A coach load of Borderers travelled from Galashiels and marched with contingents from the other regiments to the Station. We were later entertained at Redford Barracks by the Sgts Mess of 1 KOSB. The delivery of close on a million signatures to the House of Commons was the subject of much media attention and valuable publicity for our cause.

Chapter 6

The Gordons, and the Kincardine and Deeside By-Election

During the early part of the Campaign I had been aware of the efforts of Friends of the Gordon Highlanders through their letters to the national press, usually signed by Douglas Robson, their press secretary. Early in December 1991 I made contact with Douglas Robson who told me that prior to his retiral north to Deeside he had been active in the constituency of Archie Hamilton, Minister of State for the Armed Forces. He also told me that he had been in correspondence with him since "Options for Change" had been announced. He sent me copies of Archie Hamilton's letters which word for word were almost identical to the replies we had been getting from the Ministry of Defence. Archie Hamilton's letter of 14th October is reproduced here...

MINISTRY OF DEFENCE
LONDON

14th October 1991

Dear Robbie,

Thank you for your letter of 19th September. I was in fact already intending to reply to your letter of 16th September to Mr Whittingham, which had been drawn to my attention.

I know that the reduction in the number of Scottish Infantry battalions has caused much sadness, but I honestly do not share the view that we should preserve Scottish regiments simply because they are Scottish. Amalgamation has been a fact of life in the Army for many years, and most regiments are the product of amalgamation at some previous point in their existence. For example, the Gordon Highlanders themselves are the result of the amalgamation of the 75th and 92nd Regiments. In order to preserve Scottish regiments we would have had to disband or amalgamate other English or Welsh regiments with equally distinguished records. Moreover, if we had decided to retain a disproportionate number of Scottish regiments we could have been accused, not only of political bias, but of sacrificing Scottish lives in any future conflict in order to protect the English and Welsh. It is worth noting in this context that the proportion of the Infantry comprised of Scottish regiments will be about the same after restructuring as it is now.

It is, at the end of the day, an argument in which we could not hope to satisfy everybody. For that reason I am sure you will understand why I do not propose to respond to the detailed points which you raised about how the Army Board reached its decisions. Those who disagree with the conclusions might equally disagree with the way in which they are reached, but I have no doubt that the Army Board came up with the best feasible solution.

Yours ever

Archie

Archie Hamilton

D A Robson Esq, Millstream, Milton of Auchlossan Lumphanan, By Banchory, Aberdeenshire AB31 4SR.

When discussing our separate campaigns with Douglas, it became clear that a meeting between campaigners in the North and in the Borders would be constructive, for an exchange in tactics and correspondence, even although Douglas and I were reporting daily to each other by telephone. By the end of October, electioneering was in full swing for the by-election in Kincardine and Deeside. Douglas had asked all the candidates to state publicly in the press their position regarding the proposed mergers, especially the merger of the Queen's Own Highlanders and the Gordons. He was successful in soliciting responses from all the candidates in the columns of the *Deeside Piper* which are reproduced here. . .

Douglas's letter to the local Press:

The Editor
The Deeside Piper
Banchory

Dear Editor,

The recent defence debate vote showed that only two Scots Conservative MPs stood by their principles - and gave first priority to the interests and wishes of Scotland. There were other MPs who had earlier and verbally supported the retention of the Scottish Infantry regiments. They had not the will to vote accordingly. We count those and those who abstained as having acted against the Gordon Highlanders and their fellow regiments under threat.

I call upon each Parliamentary Candidate in the forthcoming Kincardine and Deeside by-election to declare in writing through the columns of the *Deeside Piper*, their solemn undertaking that in the event of their election to Parliament they shall continue to support the retention of the Gordon Highlanders and their fellow regiments under threat by every means at their disposal and that they will neither vote against nor abstain in the furtherance of that objective.

Should the *Deeside Piper* not receive such a written undertaking from any candidate, the electorate may draw their own conclusions and vote accordingly.

Yours sincerely
Douglas Robson
Press Correspondence Secretary
Friends of the Gordon Highlanders

The various replies were as follows:

NO CUTS BY THE SNP

Sir,

I am delighted to reply to DA Robson's letter by giving both my personal and the SNP's official support to the Gordon Highlanders and end the government's second-class treatment of Scottish soldiers.

The Scottish National Party is the only party with an OFFICIAL policy to save all the Scottish regiments, including the Gordons.

It is unacceptable that Scottish troops bore the brunt of the danger in the front-line in the Gulf, but are now expected to bear the brunt of the cuts.

Only SNP will scrap the Trident nuclear missile programme - which even the Navy says is totally useless - and maintain strong conventional forces.

Our policy is that every Scottish citizen serving in the British forces will be offered a place in the armed services of an independent Scotland.

No other party can square the circle of spending £23 billion on Trident AND avoid cuts in conventional forces.

It's a straight choice - troops or Trident.

Only the SNP can guarantee the future of all Scotland's regiments - including the Gordons.

Dr Allan Macartney
Scottish National Party candidate

I'LL FIGHT FOR GORDONS

Sir,

I am delighted to respond to DA Robson's letter in last week's *Piper*.

Mr Robson has done much to highlight the "Save the Gordons" campaign.

My position on the Gordon Highlanders is clear.

I have called on the Ministry of Defence to reconsider the proposed amalgamation of the Gordon Highlanders and the Queen's Highlanders.

The Conservative Party is - and always has been - the party of a strong defence for this country.

We all welcome recent long-awaited events in Eastern Europe, but the world remains an unpredictable place.

Britain's defences must remain strong and effective.

I know that the Gordons have a special place in the affections of the people of Kincardine and Deeside.

Their distinguished history has led to excellent recruitment levels, and a good retention rate.

They are amongst the most effective of regiments in our armed forces.

I am committed to fighting to ensure that the Gordons remain a distinctive part of the British Army.

Marcus Humphrey
Conservative Party

GORDONS PEACE ROLE CALL

Sir,

The Scottish Green Party does not underestimate the part the Gordon Highlanders have played in the past and we appreciate their commitment to their work.

We are not anti-Army and we are not anti-Infantry.

What we do feel is that we can not stand back and make no cuts at all while others do so in large numbers.

Given the choice the immediate target for cuts would be the cancellation of Trident followed by the removal of all our nuclear weapons.

There is much aggression in the world. The Scottish Green Party admits that world peace will not come through defence cuts alone.

We have to look at much wider issues than merely cutting arms. Let us look at two examples - Kuwait and Northern Ireland.

Twenty-eight countries were in the coalition that opposed Iraq in the Gulf War. Thirty countries, however, were in a different coalition that built up Iraq's military might in the first place.

This particular case emphasises how we must also tackle the arms trade to help reduce threats from the Saddam Husseins of this world in the future. Defence is not a single issue.

We would wish to see real commitment from the government to jobs training if the Gordons were merged and not diverting the cash to more equipment.

It would actually provide more jobs if the money saved was redirected into health, education and other sectors than the jobs lost from the merger as soldiering is capital intensive.

Mr Robson has emphasised the role of soldiers in helping out in natural disasters and similar situations.

We agree that there is a real need for a disaster relief strategy and would need specifically trained people to carry this out.

Perhaps therein lies a solution and a compromise.

If the campaigners were to accept the removal of the battalion's military function and operate as a highly trained mobile peace corps in such situations, to promote positive peace both at home and abroad then the Scottish Green Party would be happy to move to the fore of the Campaign to stop the merger.

Stephen Campbell
Scottish Green Party Candidate

MY SOLEMN UNDERTAKING

Sir,

I am happy to take up the challenge posed by Mr Robson in your paper last week, for the candidates in this by-election to give their solemn undertaking to continue to support the "Save the Gordon

Highlanders" Campaign in Parliament.

I will take pride in joining Malcolm Bruce and my other Liberal Democrat colleagues in Parliament in doing everything we can to preserve the Gordon Highlanders and the other Scottish regiments under threat.

This is indeed a 'solemn undertaking' and not the easily withdrawn vague promises the Gordon Highlanders have suffered from in the last few days.

Nicol Stephen
Liberal Democrat candidate

RESPECT FOR GORDONS

Sir,

While welcoming the increasing opportunities for international disarmament and a peace dividend, we believe that the Conservative Government's "Options for Change" was neither scientific or sensitive.

Particularly in the light of the dramatic changes in the Soviet Union subsequent of its publication.

We believe there should be a complete defence review.

We believe that in such a review the Scottish regiments would inevitably be treated more fairly, the relevance of the Infantry regiments to modern defence needs would be recognised and the historic traditions of regiments like the Gordon Highlanders would be respected.

With the Gordons' excellent record in recruitment and retention we believe that they should have a continuing opportunity to maintain the record of serving that they have shown, in the future.

I believe that the Gordons should continue as an independent regiment.

The only hope for a genuine review is the election of a Labour Government.

Malcolm Savidge
Labour Candidate

Chapter 7

Political Candidates

The day following the Kincardine and Deeside by-election, won by the Liberal Democrat, Nichol Stephen, Colonel Mike Ashmore (Royal Scots) Rtd, a Lanark farmer, and myself, in the company of two KOSB wives, Mrs Kate White and Mrs Irene Laidlaw travelled to London for the Kilroy-Silk early morning breakfast programme. Colonel Mike Ashmore managed to make several good points in favour of the Scottish regiments, and the two girls were given very good exposure, dressed in their pipers' plaids and badges. I managed to get in a reply to a Conservative MP about the by-election result, which of course the Conservatives had lost. We met campaigners from the Cheshire and Staffordshire regiments and had a useful exchange of information over breakfast. The expense of the journey and meals were all paid for by the BBC.

During the early months of the Campaign I had been struck by the pessimistic attitude of some of our serving Officers, who seemed to resent our activities, and in some cases were downright obstructive when it came to using Army property and personnel for propaganda purposes. We understood the restraints that those still serving were under, and we knew that many of them were worried about their jobs, and the future. They were under strict orders not to be involved in any debate or discussion regarding "Options for Change", and their conditions of employment precluded any involvement. What we found hard to understand was that several recently retired Officers, and some still involved with the TA were not more active in the Campaign.

It seemed to us that some of them were hell bent on wearing the new cap badge which Frank Coutts described as "St Andrew on the Cross for non payment of his Poll Tax". The first time Scottish Television asked us to produce some campaigners for interview, they asked if they could interview us against the background of the TA Centre in Galashiels where we agreed to meet. We were met with open hostility by the permanent staff who left us no doubt we would have to move on. We found this difficult to understand as the Regiment had arranged the meeting in the Officers Mess with the Local Government Officials, and even provided lunch. Regimental HQ had also been co-operative in getting us organised and even provided the initial finance from Regimental funds to get us started. Against this background it was not surprising that an atmosphere of "them and us" existed, and a certain amount of friction was generated. When the serving soldiers came to realise we were not controlled by the Army and did not give a hoot for seniority, and we came to understand the difficult position the serving Soldiers were in, relations improved greatly. In my first report to the Regiment, I stated that I was disappointed with the number of retired Officers, some of them in pensionable positions, who were prepared to stick their head above the dyke. This did not endear me to those of them with a conscience, but is was necessary to be forthright from the Campaign point of view.

One amusing incident took place involving Graham Thomson who took the majority of telephone calls in the office. A fairly senior Officer telephoned the office and Graham answered "Graham Thomson speaking" the caller asked to speak to the senior Officer to which Graham replied "there are no Officers here, we are all bloody civilians".

Mike Robson, brother of Douglas, who was Chairman of the Friends of the Gordon Highlanders Campaign, and an ex-Gordon Highlander let it be known he was prepared to stand as a candidate at the by-election. This threat, which Mike was quite prepared to carry through, caused a furore in government circles, as it was given prominent media exposure. Douglas told me of a telephone call from a prominent person in the local constituency Conservative party who asked him, "Do you intend to put up a Candidate?", Douglas asked the caller, "Why do you ask?" to which the reply came, "If you go ahead the Gordons are dead." The identity of the caller was known to Douglas, but although he has a recording of the conversation, he refuses to this day to reveal the callers' name. Grampian Television carried the story and ended their newscast by saying the Conservatives had strenuously denied the call, which made Douglas very angry.

Prior to the General election, we had a meeting of Borderers in Galashiels where thought was given to putting up candidates in key Border constituencies, like Ian Lang's Galloway and Upper Nithsdale, where Citigate had carried out a survey, much publicised in the press showing that the regimental question was uppermost in people's minds, and that the Scottish Secretary was in real danger of losing his seat, only having a majority of 1,234. *The Scotsman* carried the story that we intended putting up candidates in the regimental area, and all hell broke loose. Many senior former Borderers were horrified and telephoned to say so. It seemed that their political allegiance to the Conservative party was greater than their allegiance to the Regiment. The television networks took up the story, and the media as a whole were asking how we were to finance it. I had a long talk with the Colonel of the Regiment, Brigadier Colin Mattingley, who was opposed to the idea, but admitted it had created great interest in the Campaign. We sat with the situation for some ten days before calling a meeting in Galashiels at which it was revealed by an informed source that Tom King would not be Secretary of State for Defence following the General Election. This was one of many nods and winks we were to receive in the lead up to the Election. The following press release was issued. . .

Press release following meeting of Operation Borderer (East Borders) in Galashiels, Wednesday 20th November, 1991.

Following discussions with senior members of Keep the Scottish Battalions and speculation in the Sunday Press on an "Electoral Pact" between political parties to pressurise certain government held seats in Scotland, Operation Borderer have decided to postpone plans to field Candidates at the General Election.

Discussion with our colleagues in Dumfriesshire and the West indicate our involvement might be counterproductive, and we have no wish to embarrass Sir Hector Monro MP, who has done so much for our Campaign.

Our main aim is to ensure the survival of the King's Own Scottish Borderers as a regiment, and it is felt that enough evidence is coming out from the Defence Committee investigation to allow the government to re-assess their plans for the Scottish Battalions.

When the results of the investigation, currently proceeding, are published we will look again at the situation when government reaction is known.

It was clear to us that there was a definite Cabinet split regarding the mergers, as at the end of October Malcolm Rifkind had indicated this in a letter to Operation Borderer in which he wrote: "I have no doubt the Secretary of State for Defence will be reviewing the current proposals in the light of comments, both helpful and critical that were made during the debate in the House of Commons." He went on to say, "the amalgamations are not due to be implemented for a very considerable period of time, and therefore there will be every opportunity to give further reasoned thought to these proposals." This letter was dated the day after the Scottish Secretary Ian Lang held out similar hopes in a television debate, and was leaked to *The Scotsman* who gave it a prominent write up on 31st October 1991. Bryan Christie, the author of the *Scotsman* article, reported that the Ministry of Defence had repeated its view that there was no difference among senior ministers over the issue. The spokesman added that "changing circumstances could mean that the proposals would be reviewed in the light of comments made during the Commons debate." We were greatly encouraged by this apparent softening of attitude, as we were making no progress with our letters to Defence Secretary, Tom King, and Minister of State, Archie Hamilton. The Ministry of Defence position had not changed one bit since day one of the Campaign. Douglas Robson in the North was the first to draw blood after having a letter published in the *Daily Mail*, pointing out units were having to return to Northern Ireland twice in every 30 months, when the Ministry of Defence's target was one tour every 24 months. Archie Hamilton wrote to him criticising his letter for "an unjustified prognosis of pain and grief". We resolved to exploit the question of over-stretch and "pain and grief" to the full as it was obvious the emergency tour gap of 24 months was impossible to achieve, even before the decision to send men to Yugoslavia on "humani-tarian" duties was taken.

The Christmas parliamentary recess was used by ourselves and the Gordons to plan our strategy for the period in the lead up to the Select Committee on Defence report, due on the 6th March 1992, and the General Election in April.

Although it was clear we had much ministerial support in the Commons, and support generally in the House of Lords, the fact remained that during the October 1991 debate in the Commons only two Scottish Conservative MPs, Sir Nicholas Fairbairn, and Sir Hector Monro, plus five English Conservative MPs had voted against the government. It was also remembered that the impas-sioned speech by Shirley Finlay-Maxwell at the Conservative Party Conference in the Autumn of 1991, whilst getting the largest ovation of the Conference, failed to win the debate.

We had to attack on two fronts, through the Members of Parliament and the media, and this we set about doing early in January 1992.

Severin Carrell, the *Scotsman* defence correspondent, who had been working on the Regimental story for some months, managed at last to get an interview with Armed Forces Minister Archie Hamilton, in his office at the Ministry of Defence. Severin managed to get him to admit that politics had played a large part in how regiments had been selected for amalgamation. Severin Carrell's report revealed that in an exclusive interview Archie Hamilton had conceded that the political need to maintain a spread of Regiments throughout Britain had weighed against keeping the Scottish Infantry Division intact. Defence Ministers had previously refused to concede a political element in their decisions and had even rejected demands from the select commitee to release documents which explained how regiments were selected for amalgamation. In his interview, Archie Hamilton said, "Recruitability is one consideration. Quite clearly the Army finds it more difficult to recruit form the south-east (of England) than it does from the north-east and from Scotland. Nobody would deny that." But he dismissed as inaccurate the analogy made by one campaigner that the choice of regiments being cut was similar to a supermarket chain cutting its most profitable stores in favour of less profitable shops. "If you take you analogy right through, you would end up with a seriously large number of regiments in Scotland, and the north-east and north-west, and probably none south of a line drawn across the Wash. Now that is not politically acceptable, and the people in the south would resent it, and resent it bitterly."

The Scotsman also devoted its editorial comment to the Archie Hamilton interview, and concluded, "It is to Mr Hamilton's credit that he admits that it is the last consideration (decisions made in the best interests of the country at large) which really counts. When in considering reducing the number of regiments, everything else had been thrown into the pot - geography, demography, recruitability - politics decided the issue. The Scots regiments, in short, suffered proportionately more because the Government had less to lose north of the Border."

This was major breakthrough and solicited several letters to the Editor, including one from the Minister himself. This was the first time a Minister had admitted that the Scottish Division's ability to recruit and retain men was an important matter.

Chapter 8

Operation Borderer Phase 2

Phase 2 of Operation Borderer was launched in Ednam House Hotel in Kelso following the funeral of Major Edward Atkinson who had been very active in the Campaign. Brigadier Allan Alstead drafted the orders for Phase 2 of the Campaign. They were faxed to RHQ and issued as a press release on 30th January 1992 as follows.

OPERATION BORDERER - PHASE 2

SITUATION
1. Phase 1 of the Campaign may not have managed to get the government to change its plans to amalgamate the Scottish regiments, but it has made the Cabinet well aware how unpopular and ill-conceived its plans are. There are indications that ministers would like to make changes, but there needs to be a credible excuse for going back on their earlier decision. Even more important is to recognise that the political situation will change after the General Election and we know that Tom King will not continue in Defence should the Conservatives get back into office.

2. A new Conservative Secretary of State for Defence could change amalgamation plans without any loss of political face.

Should Labour get back into power then they must be convinced of the justice of our cause; the same applies to the Liberal Democrats as they could hold the balance of power in a new House of Commons.

MISSION
3. In the run-up to the General Election, Borderers are now to increase the pressure to retain the KOSB as an unamalgamated regiment.

EXECUTION
4. General Outline
We must keep the public aware of the defence issues and the debate must be continued with vigour in the media and by letter. Following the great success of the petition, the Campaign has slowed down so we must make it clear we are still very much in business. The first step is to react in an effective manner to the work of the Commons Select Committee on Defence and the second is to step up the second phase of our Campaign as soon as a date for the General Election is announced.

ACTION PLAN
5. Select Committee on Defence
The Commons Select Committee on Defence has been meeting and this body needs to be bombarded with letters stressing the problems that will result from the planned cuts in the number of battalions. News of the deliberations of this committee must therefore be carefully monitored and our reactions given maximum publicity, particularly if the Conservatives close ranks before the election to present a bland, uncritical final report. The last scheduled meeting of the Committee was on 15th January and there will be further meetings before it presents its final report which is due mid-February. Write to the Chairman, Michael Mates MP, to press our case and reinforce opposition to

the cuts based on a firm strategic, not emotional, approach. Write also to any Select Committee member - the more the better.

6. General Election Campaign
The candidates from the main parties should be known by everyone in their own constituency - write to them all to seek their unreserved support for the Campaign to save the Regiment. Results of this can be co-ordinated in the East and West Regimental area and presented to the media as a 'guide' for those who wish to cast their vote in support of the Regiment.

7. Regimental Parliamentary Candidate
No parliamentary candidates will be sponsored by the Regiment, or by the Keep Our Scottish Battalions Campaign. The threat worked to the extent intended for the Gordons, but all regiments are agreed that to put forward candidates would be counter-productive.

8. Opinion Survey
The KOSB Campaign is planning possibly to conduct a survey in the areas of the four affected regiments using the British Legion net.

9. Media Statements
Indications are from the media that there is still a lot of interest in the Campaign. Think of new ideas and fresh approaches - make our Campaign lively - not boring! A regular flow of comment to the media must be maintained therefore and steadily increased in intensity as the General Election gets closer. Give good stories to other regiments to use on a wider network. This will be co-ordinated by Donald Fairgrieve in the East and William Turner in the West. For general statements about Operation Borderer, Brigadier Frank Coutts and Bob Riddle are available.

10. Letter Writing

A further barrage of letters will be needed from everyone and aimed at all levels, from the Prime Minister down to Party Parliamentary Candidates. A number of points which can be used in letters is attached. The importance of letters from all parts of the UK cannot be overstressed and therefore the contribution which can be made by Association/Officers Club/Friends in England or overseas is a key factor.

11. Meetings/Rallies

There may be scope for holding meetings or rallies on an East and West basis nearer the date of the General Election.

CO-ORDINATING INSTRUCTIONS

12. Dates and times will depend on the announcement of the General Election date.

13. The excellent, well tried organisation that carried through the petition will continue with Donald Fairgrieve in the East and William Turner in the West as the co-ordinators.

14. Further discussions are taking place on whether to continue to use Westminster Communications to press our case in London and in the national media.

Chapter 9

Defence Select Committee Report
and the General Election

The long awaited all-Party Defence Committee report published on 6th March gave us much ammunition in the lead up the General Election. It echoed all we had been saying about over-stretch and the unfairness of the selection for amalgamation. It was very critical of Ministers' reluctance to supply information needed for an accurate assessment of the situation. The *Scotsman* devoted its editorial on 7th March to the report with the headline "Defence Strategy Under Fire" and went on to say. . .

The Select Committee on Defence has written few reports in recent years more keenly awaited or more politically sensitive within the Conservative Party than that published yesterday on the government's proposed cuts in the Army. The committee is dominated by Conservatives; chaired by a senior and respected Conservative back-bencher, it also includes two former Conservative junior defence ministers. They, with their Labour colleagues, have been critically investigating an issue extremely dear to the party's heart - the national defence.

Meanwhile, the pre-general election hostilities have been heating up. Several weeks ago, it was reported that Tory whips were lobbying their colleagues on the committee to tone down criticism of the government, and to put party above parliament. The committee did not.

Its report 'Options for Change: Army—Review of the White Paper, Britain's Army for the 90s', not only challenges the government's arithmetic but accuses ministers both of haphazard decision-making and also of failing to allow effective scrutiny of that process by refusing to supply the information needed for an accurate assessment of the issue.

Consequently, the committee complains it has been unable to reach clear conclusions on the fairness of the way regiments, and the four Scottish regiments in particular, were selected for amalgamation. Given the lack of detailed official information the committee could only note that "the fact remains that several of the best recruited regiments from north of the Wash are being amalgamated whilst certain others are not."

Although the committee makes clear there is no direct evidence that the Army will be unable to fulfil its formal war-time commitments as currently predicted, it concludes that with the very tight margin for error in the government's arithmetic, any unexpected war or peacekeeping operation could quite easily expose Options inadequacies.

Despite ministerial protests that their calculations have been careful and considered, this tough analysis by the select committee paints a picture of ministerial decision-making and accountability which is not encouraging, particularly during such unpredictable times.

The government's unwavering defence of its position may be politically expedient before a general election, but its refusal to allow full and complete scrutiny of its decisions or admit to the widely-held view that the cuts were strongly influenced by the Treasury, suggest they may really be uncertain of their case. Indeed, the growing clamour from all the political parties for a reappraisal of the cuts, as proposed by the select committee, deserves far more respect than has yet been given.

A list of all the Scottish MPs was drawn up and letters were sent to all 72. As replies came in, we updated our list with information as to whether MPs were supportive or not. We also sent out a letter to all the Conservative Constituency Offices in Scotland as follows. . .

Fountainhead Cottage
Sunderland Hall
Galashiels
TD1 3PG

14th February 1992

As the General Election approaches, many people are making up their minds how to vote. Under "Options for Change" the Conservative Government propose to cut our Infantry Battalions beyond the limits of safety. This will have a particularly detrimental effect on Scottish life, as our Scottish Battalions are part of the fabric of life in Scotland, with family connections going back generations.

The All Party Committee on Defence have been extremely critical of the cuts, which Archie Hamilton has admitted to *The Scotsman* are political. Many Conservative members have either resigned or suspended membership, and unless pressure is brought to bear for a review of the proposals, many thousands of votes will be lost. Over 800,000 people signed the petition to Parliament to Save Our Scottish Battalions. Please make sure your Conservative Candidate is aware of the situation, and ask that they write to the Secretary of State at the Scottish Office, informing him of the strength of feeling on the subject. The news that 1200 men are to be sent to assist the UN in Yugoslavia will exacerbate an already dangerous overstretch of our Infantry Battalions.

WD Fairgrieve
Operation Borderer (East)

As the General Election Campaign began to gain momentum, it was clear that here we had an opportunity to gain valuable publicity for the Campaign. We decided to set up a telephone line with several lines so that voters could phone-in to ask how any particular candidate stood on the Regimental question. Letters were sent out to all candidates asking them to return signed statements of how they stood, including whether they would vote against the government if required, on the amalgamations. . .

Fountainhead Cottage
Sunderland Hall
Galashiels
TD1 3PG

27th March 1992

You will no doubt be aware that we are running a telephone line from 1st April 1992 until 9th April 1992, to assist the many thousands of KOSB supporters to make up their minds how to cast their vote in support of the Regiment.

We are asking all the candidates to answer the questions on the enclosed slip and sign it, as we want to be fair to all concerned. Please return the slip either to the above address or to 41 Bank Street, Galashiels, before Wednesday 1st April 1992.

Operation Borderer take this opportunity to wish you good luck in the coming Election.

Yours sincerely
WD Fairgrieve
(Operation Borderer)

A list of phone numbers of members of Operation Borderer in six Border towns was then given.

OPERATION BORDERER PHONE LINE
1st April 1992 to 9th April 1992

1. In view of the findings of the Select Committee on Defence will your Party order a review of the Defence cuts under "Options for Change"?

2. If elected will you strenuously campaign for the retention of the KOSB as an unamalgamated Regiment, including voting against the Government of the day if necessary?

Signed .... Dated ....

The Gordons in the north decided to do the same thing and a network of telephone numbers was established in both areas. The media took up the story, not only locally but nationally with radio and television clamouring for details. Advertisements were placed in the local press giving details of the phone numbers and the times they were manned.

The Conservative candidates in the Borders reacted straight away and Lloyd Beat in Ettrick and Lauderdale went on the radio to say we were playing with fire, and could be prosecuted under the Representation of the People Act, for trying to influence voting. Many prominent Conservatives telephoned me to try and dissuade us from running the "phone in". At the same time we revealed that several business people were supporting us financially instead of sending their usual contribution to the Conservative Party. Severin Carrell of *The Scotsman* gave prominent treatment to the story which is reproduced here. . .

ARMY CUTS OPPONENTS TARGET TORY DONATIONS
By Severin Carrell

Leading Scots businessmen who fund the Conservative Party are being asked by regimental campaigners to approach the Prime Minister and other cabinet ministers privately on their behalf.

Contacts between senior campaign figures and business leaders are expected to remain low key at first, but campaigners are prepared to ask business contacts to threaten funding of the party as a last resort.

The move follows several warnings last year by Scottish campaigners, particularly in the north-east, that they would call on companies to withdraw funds from the Tories unless regiments earmarked for merger were reprieved.

English anti-merger campaigners have won the support of several influential Tory party donors.

Leaders of Keep Our Scottish Battalions, which is fighting to save at least two of the four Scots regiments being merged, had refused to resort to that tactic.

It feared it would antagonise the government and lose Conservative Party support. But campaigners claim that after the government failed to use several key opportunities to reprieve the regiments last year, a direct challenge is required.

With the Commons Defence Select Committee expected to publish a report next week on the regimental cuts which is heavily critical of the government, pro-regiment campaigns in Scotland and the Midlands will exploit the opportunity to increase pressure on the government.

Donald Fairgrieve, a spokesman for Operation Borderer, the group fighting the amalgamation of the King's Own Scottish Borderers with the Royal Scots, said yesterday that the group had drawn up a list of a dozen large Borders firms backing the Conservatives. Several leading knitwear and woollens companies on the list are being approached, he said, as are companies which generously support the Conservatives but also funded Operation Borderer.

It is uncertain how donors would react to a move which could damage the Tories' electoral chances, but with party leaders appealing for election-fighting funds, Mr Fairgrieve claimed: "Anything that inhibits that is going to have an influence".

Mike Robson said a number of "Dear John" letters will be sent to the Prime Minister saying "Look, we are, as you probably know, a big subscriber to Conservative Party funds. We are most perturbed and uneasy about what the government are proposing to do with the defence cuts".

He said he would support any company which went beyond this implied threat of withholding funds by reducing or suspending its donation.

BBC Television London picked up on the 'phone line' and sent a television crew from London to film us in action. We quickly set up an Operations Room in the upstairs lounge of the Salmon Inn in Galashiels. We obtained six telephones from British Telecom which were ranged along a tartan covered table, and manned by volunteers. We explained to the BBC our lines were not open until 6.30pm which they accepted. This was just as well as none of the phones were connected, the real lines were in our homes in various Border Towns. The BBC team were very interested in the financial contributions given to us, rather than the Conservative Party, and were most anxious to interview one or more of the businesses concerned. We refused to divulge names which rather put them off the 'phone line' story. The phone lines opened on the 1st April and we took over 300 calls, some of which we recognised as Party workers who were wondering what we were saying. The Gordons phone line was also a great success generating much media attention.

The Conservative Party had set up a telephone line in London, and Charlie Laidlaw organised for calls from all the various Regimental areas. We in the Borders telephoned round as many of our supporters as we could muster urging them to telephone asking questions on defence and in particular on the cuts under Options for Change. After two days and several hundred calls we were diverted to a Ministry of Defence spokesman who tried to deal with all our calls. The Gordons and the Queen's Own Highlanders organised similar activity in the north and the Royal Scots in Edinburgh. We were successful in jamming up the London line for two days. This all helped to keep up the momentum we had built up in the run up to the General Election. Simon Nayyar of Westminster Communications, who had been retained to "lobby" on our behalf at a cost of £1500 per month, was seconded to Conservative Central Office for the period of the election. Simon was forced to go AWOL for 48 hours when the debate turned to defence. The government were clearly rattled by our perseverance and wanted to sweep the Regimental question under the carpet. We were twice told by Ministers that if we dropped the Campaign they would consider reprieves.

After the General Election in April, ways and means of keeping the Campaign in the public eye were discussed, and we decided to hold another Rally in Galashiels to mark one year of Operation Borderer. We resolved to make the Rally a national effort and involve all the regiments under threat of amalgamation. The date was fixed for Saturday 22nd August and we set about involving as many bands and local organisations as possible. At the end of May a meeting was held in the Isle of Skye Hotel, Perth which was attended by Hamish Logan, Charlie Laidlaw (Citigate), Michael Robson and myself.

Charlie Laidlaw reported in some detail where the Campaign stood and said that we had made significant progress with the politicians, but that progress with the Ministry of Defence was non-existent. Hamish Logan reported that General Sir John MacMillan had written to all Scottish MPs and his letter is reproduced here. . .

Chapter 10

The Chairman's Letter to Scottish MPs and to General Sir Peter Inge CGS

To all Scottish MPs (except Mr Rifkind)

Boghall Farm
Thornhill
Stirling
FK8 3QD

2nd June 1993

I wrote recently to you as Parliament reassembled after the General Election, and have had a number of responses, showing that the support which existed several months ago is in no way diminished. Thank you very much for your encouragement.

One suggestion that has been made by a number of our supporters in Parliament is that a delegation of Scottish MPs and possibly Peers as well, should call on Malcolm Rifkind and repeat the message that we were trying to get through to Tom King. I have discouraged this at the present time for two reasons. First, Malcolm Rifkind was so interested in the most detailed briefings which he received before he took up this appointment that it would be insulting to suggest to him that he did not know why we were continuing our Campaign. Secondly, I asked Hector

Monro to sound him out privately to find out whether he would prefer that we followed in the footsteps of the Staffords and others, or if he would appreciate it if we left him to get on with his studies of the problems in the new Department on which he will eventually make some important judgements. He emphatically said that he needed time, and that he does not propose in any case to make any hurried changes. It therefore seemed likely to prejudice our position of being understanding supporters of a natural ally if we went along as third in the queue and were given pretty short shift.

But there is a third reason why I do not think it would be right to hassle him just now. This is because all the rumours that reach me suggest that it is not the Minister but the military members of the Army Board who are dragging their heels. I have therefore written the enclosed letter to the CGS, hoping that he will have the confidence to do something about asking for more Infantry, instead of frittering away the goodwill that exists in such a degree at present by seeking to make up a great many less spectacular deficiencies in the proposed Army for the Nineties.

You may find the arguments helpful when posing Parliamentary Questions, or when lobbying the Service Ministers, or better still their Civil Servants and advisers.

I believe the programme for the next month or two should be like water dripping on a stone, and I would be most grateful if you would take any official or unofficial opportunity to continue to make these points. I expect a recognisable point will arise when we should raise the chorus once more in a co-ordinated way, and I would be glad to know of any forthcoming events that you can identify which would give us the chance to make a major issue. We need to conserve our power to some extent so that the impact is that much greater when we open fire - but we don't want to be left with a pile of shot and the battle over.

We have one advantage over many divisions. The Scottish amalgamations come late in the day. If no reprieve is given before other viable units go to the wall, then when the penny at last drops we will be even better placed to gain from the new Age of Enlightenment, which surely must dawn despite the Army Board. I hope we can play this to our advantage also.

Yours sincerely
John MacMillan
Lieutenant General Sir John MacMillan

To General Sir Peter Inge CGS

Boghall Farm
Thornhill
Stirling
FK8 3QD

18 June 1992

You have good reason to be fed up with people trying to tell you how to run your affairs, but I owe it to my fellow campaigners to fire one more shot in your direction. I am sorry if I am joining the queue of bores, but the stakes are high and I would not be forgiven if I let the case go by default, particularly as I am trying to dissuade our political lobby from taking up more of Malcolm Rifkind's valuable time at present.

I feel the need to write because rumour has reached me from a number of directions that the Army's attitude to any add-back is that the Infantry would come very low on the list of priorities. It would be most unlikely to benefit at all once the other items on the shopping list have been met. I have even heard that there are staff officers in MO who believe that emergency tour intervals will be 29 months 'once everything settles down'. I believe it is therefore important to restate the case for some increase in the size of the Infantry post-'Options', and for you to be reminded of the case for some of that increase being drawn from Scotland.

A Viable Infantry Army

The Infantry in our tiny future Army must have the level of expertise that you will expect of all other Arms for the All Arms battle and Joint Service operations as well as the peacekeeping skills that are so demanding in time at present, and which may well become even more important if we are to hold our heads up in Europe. Failure to achieve a proper level of competence will undoubtedly prejudice the chances of the ARRC ever being recognised as a better option than the Franco-German alternative. But viable Infantry depends upon its officers, soldiers, and above all senior ranks believing that their dedication is appreciated and that they have time to meet all their tasks professionally as well as having the opportunity to enjoy a reasonable quality of life.

Emergency Tour Intervals

At the heart of the equation is the interval between Emergency Tours. When the Army Board set the 24 month target, the standard tour in Northern Ireland was 4 months. The six month tour crept in against the better judgement of many people closely concerned with operations, and yet the 24 month target was not extended to match the increased period of operations. The resilience of units who have had considerably shorter intervals has largely been achieved by the variety in their lives when they have been away from the Northern Ireland treadmill, in Hong Kong, Cyprus, Berlin, or even when their unaccompanied tours have been in stations like Belize where the dangers have been less worrying to the wives and girl-friends.

Northern Ireland

When you and I were privileged to serve in Northern Ireland the expertise of the IRA was still developing, there was a degree of novelty in the experience, and above all we had the chance to put our own stamp in a campaign which was led by the Army. There were plenty of frustrations, a degree of danger, and, for the Emergency Tour units in particular, a considerable amount of deprivation. We threw ourselves into it, and came home slimmer and probably fairly knackered, just in time to be told we were going back six months later. We probably had Gunners to the left of us and Cavalry to the right, and we had little but rifles and common sense as our weapons. I needn't remind you that it has moved on a long way since then, but the particular points that must be made are that it is no longer a game for amateurs, and the Infantry are the experts; it is experts who will win the campaign if anyone can. Secondly, the other Arms cannot afford a year away from their primary of slack there - and it is wasteful to let their expensively learnt skills deteriorate for lack of practice on their role. Thirdly, RUC primacy undoubtedly increases the feeling of frustration among all ranks in comparison with the time when a unit's successes or failures could be task - or if they can we must be budgeting for a great deal laid at its own door, and the risks its soldiers were asked to take were largely of its own making: this has an impact on the frequency of tours, particularly for Senior Ranks.

Long Service NCOs and Senior Ranks
The backbone of our regular units is the corps of Warrant Officers, Senior Ranks and long service Corporals. These are the people who will feel the shrinking horizons of the Army of the Nineties to the greatest degree. The variety of battalion postings is becoming more restricted: the chance for service away from the unit scarcely occurs below sergeant, and the diminishing ITO will probably accentuate this. If the womenfolk drag their men out because they see them constantly returning for further tours of Northern Ireland whilst they sit at home and worry, we will have an Army no better than our Continental Allies, but a fraction of their size. If small is to be better then the career pattern of the men who are to be the Warrant Officers of the future must be not only tolerable but attractive.

Peacekeeping Duties
I have said a good deal about Northern Ireland, but the collapse of the Soviet empire has put a completely new face on the roles of the Services

73

throughout the Western world. While we must not discount the possibility of conventional war on a scale such as Saddam Hussein thrust upon us so unexpectedly, the tasks facing the UN and EC servicemen in Yugoslavia are only one example of the need for people who are skilled and experienced in peacekeeping operations to be ready to play their part in helping nations to live together without slaughtering each other. This in turn brings the miseries of starvation in their trail, as is happening from the Black Sea to Central Africa. Britain has already had egg on its face because the only contingent we could muster for Yugoslavia was a field ambulance, excellent though that is in humanitarian terms. With the full impact of the Chapple/King plan still to take effect any pretence of being 'at the heart of Europe' will look pretty stupid in military terms if we cannot do better the next time a call for peacekeepers arises. When there is still talk of replacement for the RAF's nuclear weapon, as well as our investment in Trident at four boats being considered essential to our future safety one wonders if the planners are living in to-day's world or one of their own. We already have a peacekeeping campaign unresolved, as well as others on the horizon, yet that is the area where the cuts are falling.

The Infantry Mix
With so few battalions to meet the task in Northern Ireland it can only have been to honour the political pledge to Nepal that resources were earmarked for the remaining Gurkha units. Similarly the mathematics of three Parachute Battalions to provide two in role, (and consequently of limited availability for peacekeeping at home) are hard to assess without more knowledge than we can have outside the system. Could not the reverse of the existing system of secondment into the Parachute Brigade have provided the variety that they need in a more flexible way? But be that as it may, restricted availability of the units that will remain must place a heavier burden on those which are fully adaptable. If add-back should arise then it is essential that it goes to units with the full range of operational capability.

Parliament's Views

The House of Commons Select Committee on Defence, a very large number of constituency MP's, often with no connection with affected regiments, and many distinguished Peers have expressed their approval for the Options package as a whole, but have been outspoken in their criticism of the impact of the cuts on the Infantry. You have a powerful alliance which crosses party lines, waiting to support you if you ask for more resources from the government to increase the strength of the Infantry. They can override the Civil Service, who are concerned that Defence will not get a larger slice of the cake, but there is very little likelihood that they would give you anything but lukewarm support if you asked for extra signallers or establishment enhancements in less high profile units, unless you bid generously for the Infantry as your top priority. This is an opportunity that is most unlikely to recur, and should be seized before your supporters give up their pressure in despair at the Army's apparent lack of interest.

Full Strength Battalions

One of the arguments used frequently by Tom King and John Major when replying to letters from correspondents on this subject was that many of the overstretch problems were caused by understrength battalions. After Options the Infantry would have no difficulty retaining full manning. You know as well as I do that the movement of the slide rule does not make the difference between a weak unit and a strong one in the Infantry. Why have most of the large regiments so signally failed since the last amalgamations? (*Pace* Dwin Bramall!) You can only go by the record, which is based on far more influences than demography, not least among them being the relative value of the military salary and the livelihood that can be gained by staying at home. It merely illustrated the shallowness of the thought of Tom King's writers when the full strength battalions argument was sent to representatives of full strength battalions which are scheduled for amalgamation.

Scotland's Position

The record of the Scottish Division in manning terms has been the best of all the Line Divisions over many years. It has suffered, as have most others, from the effects of Recruit Capping, as well as the uncertainty hanging over four of the battalions which are to be affected by amalgamation. Yet it remains the strongest Division, with a healthy complement of young officers also still joining an organisation where competition will be intense and the future structure uncertain. Should Second Scots Guards be amalgamated, as planned, there would not be the slightest difficulty in maintaining the strength of the eight Infantry battalions recruiting in Scotland for the foreseeable future. Even with nine battalions to support the prospects are good if the threat of amalgamation is withdrawn.

Conclusion

The world is in a state of uncertainty where trained Infantry will be at a premium.

You have an opportunity to cash in on the goodwill of Lords and Commons to gain an enhancement for the Infantry.

You need full strength Infantry units.

Scotland provides them now, in so far as you permit us. Scotland can do so in the future.

Post Script

The names of Fraser and Beach were maligned for trying to make bricks without straw in the BAOR reorganisation.

King and Chapple will go down similarly in history.

Rifkind and Inge have the opportunity to redeem the situation.

Yours

John

General Sir Peter Inge KCB
Chief of The General Staff
Ministry of Defence, Whitehall, London

Chapter 11

Memo Found by New Minister of Defence

Operation Borderer RHQ,
KOSB
The Barracks
Berwick upon Tweed
TD15 1DG

MEMO FOUND IN OFFICE BY
NEW MINISTER OF DEFENCE

Dear M,

Well done on promotion. Fear defence policy in disarray. No time for a review. Only choice - obey Treasury. Called plans "Options" to make it appear we had studied all angles! Despite no philosophy, or data bank of facts. Secretariat has done great job answering mail - most from you stroppy Scots - with red herrings. Our forces are reduced to sticking fingers in the dyke, through which are pouring Arabs, Kurds, Serbs, etc. Must not take on any UN tasks.

RN good hands - Falklands improved their moral greatly - so I have OK'd 4th Trident. Don't understand argument that other three won't work without it, but need the jobs anyway. Pity Barrow did not reward us in Election. Dearly hope Democrats don't reach White House. I foresee circumstances when not even Bush will give us the missiles - v. embarrassing!

RAF did a great job in the Gulf, so I have supported EFA despite German rumblings. Have set up a cell to justify it, but as yet no success. Sure you will think up something.

The only way to reduce Army budget effectively was to hammer the cavalry and the infantry. Sure I was right to single out Scots regiments, and save those in our dodgy seats in N. of England, despite their manning problems. Pity about Linda, but she will look decorative in the Lords. Glad to see you Jocks got back in despite my plan.

Found the Select Committee too difficult, so refused to give evidence. Hope the PM has sense to give the Colonel and Sir Hector jobs, to keep them quiet.

Good luck - I am looking forward to getting back to my farm. Have you got some good shooting on the Pentlands?

Yours ever

T.Rex

13th April 1992

We discussed the lack of communication between the various parts of the Campaign and agreed this could be improved. It was decided that a monthly SITREP would be sent out to all Regimental representatives. Charlie Laidlaw agreed to help with the publicity for the Galashiels Rally, where his press contacts would be invaluable.

Chapter 12

Amalgamation Decisions
and Proposed Cap Badge

I was rather depressed on my return from the Perth meeting to find a letter from Regimental HQ regarding the amalgamation planning decisions signed by the Colonel of the Regiment. We had all realised that the amalgamation planning was going on, but the letter brought it home to us that time was running out. The planning committee seemed to have got on rather well, and as Frank Coutts remarked were pursuing their task with too much enthusiasm for his liking.

Regimental Headquarters
The King's Own Scottish Borderers
The Barracks
Berwick-upon-Tweed
TD15 1DG

AMALGAMATION PLANNING DECISIONS

TITLE: The Royal Scots Borderers (The Royal Regiment)
TARTAN: Leslie - Royal Stuart for pipers - Hunting Stuart for drummers
CAP BADGE: A new Capbadge to be designed. To incorporate the New Title - Initial consideration to be given to incorporating the RS 1878

design with the KOSB castle, as a basis for development - Collar dogs would be the Castle - Buttons would incorporate the new capbadge design.

It was agreed that Joint Sub Committee drawn from the respective Regimental Headquarters and 1st Battalions would make recommendations on all other aspects of dress and ancillaries.

These decisions of the Amalgamation Committee are subject to the agreement of the Colonel in Chief (Designate) of the new Regiment. All aspects of the amalgamation will require various stages of sanctions by Ministry of Defence Committees. The major ones are then submitted for gracious acceptance by HM The Queen before formal promulgation.

The appointment of Malcolm Rifkind to Defence in the new Cabinet, gave great encouragement to all involved in the Keep Our Scottish Battalions Campaign as we knew he was broadly sympathetic to our cause, and that he had been well briefed by both regiments, particularly by the brothers Ian and Stuart McBain in Edinburgh. We were also pleased that the information we had received saying that Tom King would not be at Defence after the Election was correct.

General Sir John MacMillan through Charlie Laidlaw let it be known that we were to leave the Minister of Defence alone until he settled in, and took stock of his inherited position. This we did, although we continued to write to the MoD in the person of Mr JB Stainton, Assistant Private Secretary to the Minister. Both Douglas Robson and I had been writing regularly to Mr Stainton, who either did not address our questions, or repeated the same old tired answers, especially on the overstretching of our Infantry Battalions. He refused to give an answer to our question as to why certain well recruited regiments had been selected for amalgamation while others 11% undermanned had not. He persisted in his claim that a two year gap between emergency tours was attainable when the amalgamations were completed,

The launch of "Keep Our Scottish Battalions", on Calton Hill 21st August 1991. Brigadier Frank Coutts (right) speaks to Regimental Secretary Colonel Colin Hogg (left) and Major Willie Turner.

Lt General Sir John MacMillan fires the first salvo.

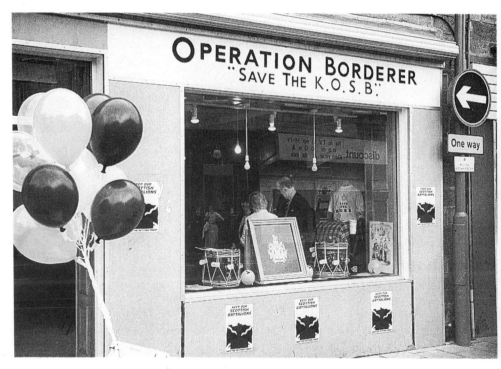

The Operation Borderer Office in Galashiels.

Local Butcher Jim Cockburn hands over a cheque to Graham Thomson and Jack Scott.

Petition gathering at the Selkirk Sevens—Pipe Major David Bunyan,
Donald Fairgrieve and David Hartley.

Drum Major Jock Lyall makes a point to a BBC Cameraman.

First Galashiels Rally. Left to right——Colonel of the Regiment, Brigadier Frank Coutts, Sir Nicholas Fairbairn QC MP, Archie Kirkwood MP, and Sir David Steel MP.

The public join the march. Lorraine Walker (centre) and Morag Coutts (far right).

Dumfries Rally—Messrs Seaton, Davis, Paterson and Wilson (kneeling).

Graham Thomson asks: "Who stole my pie?"

Korean Veterans Minden Day, Glencorse.

Father and Son—Colonels Colin and Donald Hogg
with Muir Sturrock and Jeremy Ballantyne.

A Section of the Rally in Scott Park, Galashiels.

Ian Lang shakes hands with Brigadier Frank Coutts, Borders Regional HQ.

Sir David Steel addresses the Rally flanked by (left to right) John Home-Robertson MP,
Alistair Hutton, Lt General Sir John MacMillan and Winifred Ewing MP.

A Section of the Borderers contingent—Edinburgh Rally.

The Staffords Mascot, Edinburgh Rally, which went through the entire parade without lifting its leg!

St Cuthbert's Church Hall—Edinburgh Rally.

Lonnach Pipe Band, described by *The Times* as "wild men from the hills".

We did it! Donald and Pat Fairgrieve with Willie Turner.

The 1st Battalion say thank you. Galashiels, 3rd April 1993.

Major Willie Turner and helpers at the Victory Celebration,
Dumfries, 26th February 1993.

1st Battalion march past; Galashiels 3rd April 1993.

Colonel John Kirkwood accepts slate, watched by Brigadier & Mrs Alstead
and Charlie Laidlaw.

when it was clear to us that 18 months and even 15 months was the norm, before any amalgamations had taken place. This was a strong card in our favour, and we kept labouring the point in all our correspondence with MPs and the MoD. In the end, they had to admit they were wrong, to the Select Committee on Defence. The media made much of this climb down and it gave further strength to our case.

Chapter 13

The Army Presentation Team

On the 14th May, Michael Hall and I travelled to Hamilton's Bothwell Bridge Hotel to attend the Army Presentation Team's PR lecture on the role of the modern Army. The team had already performed in the Cowdray Hall in Aberdeen on the 7th May attended by the Robson brothers. We were fully briefed by Douglas Robson who sent me his thoughts on the presentation the following day. They were. . .

The Army Presentation Team
The Cowdray Hall
Aberdeen 7th May 1992

These are my recollections and impressions, set down the following day.

1) Audience, about 30 persons out of uniform; some were certainly serving officers. There were 3-4 ladies also attending.

2) The audio-visual presentation was "glossy". The 3 speakers were proficient. The whole presentation was a scarcely disguised piece of propaganda on behalf of "Options for Change" and partly similar to a recruiting film, partly "showing the flag" - ie "let's keep the civvies

happy about what's going on".

3) The Brigadier who introduced the team virtually said "This presentation is about how "Options for Change" - which is irreversible, other than "fine tuning" if and as changing circumstances warrant it - affect the Army, how it is adapting itself to this and the changed circumstances, how the Army is rehabilitating those who are leaving - either voluntarily or compulsory." He also more or less stated that the Team would not answer questions regarding "Options for Change" decisions.

4) Perhaps discouraged by that last remark - or because apathy was ringing through the attendees, there were only 4 questioners; a lady (hardly audible) who, I think, was asking questions on redundancy terms/rehabilitation. An ex-Gordon (elderly) who was asking about the rehousing of redundant soldiers, and pointing out the local housing shortages, prices and employment difficulties. Mike Robson and Douglas Robson who asked between them - because no-one else spoke up - virtually all the 9 questions on the list I had produced (not necessarily in the same words as written). Additionally, I suggested that the Army could live to regret the fact that the men they were cutting were the equivalent of "middle management" in Industry - and that Industry had suffered badly when they had done the same some years ago. (The Colonel seemed to be particularly interested in this point.)

5) The Colonel vehemently denied that regiments were being sent to Ulster at intervals less than 24 months. He said that he had just checked on the point. He challenged us to name regiments (Mike did).

6) The Colonel said that it was NOT the politicians who had planned "Options for Change" - it was "the centre". When I queried what was meant by "the centre" - was it the Treasury AND/OR Civil Servants? he said it was senior Army Officers. When I asked how it was that thousands of distinguished and very experienced serving and retired

83

officers were so much opposed to the Infantry cuts, the answer was that they were not so up-to-date with or aware of the changing circumstances!

7) I had put several other points to the Colonel prior to the presentation in perhaps 10 minutes of discussion (points taken from our usual ones). After the presentation I managed to do likewise with the Brigadier. He admitted much more of the correctness of our questioning, in this "private" session, than either he or the Colonel had during the formal presentation. I pointed out that all the time the Colonel had been "denying" our points about the regiments/men being understrength/ over committed, he had nevertheless been using, frequently, the words "stretched", "overstretched" in his talk/answers. The Brigadier admitted to this. I had asked if the Army wanted a stable, constant, high level of trained seasoned infantrymen - a predictable strength - available to them? (During the question period.) The Colonel had replied that obviously they did. I had then asked if this could not be best achieved by drawing mainly from the best recruited and retained regiments. The Colonel had replied that it was not only the Scottish regiments that were well recruited - many were; we should not adopt the attitude that cuts and amalgamation were OK if they were not applied in one's own back yard. He refused to be drawn into further discussion on the point of selection of regiments either for achieving the make-up of the required Infantry or selected for "the chop". However, referring to that point, after the presentation (and during our "private" session, the Brigadier made a particular point of stressing that we, the Gordons, were not fully up to strength, and that we should do everything possible to rectify this, as there was no doubt that, in the event that there would be any "add-back", they would most certainly do it on the basis of looking at the record of the regiments in recruiting and retaining a full strength position. (Incidentally, the Brigadier claimed not to know anything of Archie Hamilton's statement/s in *The Scotsman* - about "The Scottish regiments undoubtedly have the best record," etc.)

8) Michael gave the Colonel our written list of 9 questions, with the request that these be put to the Army Board, and that we receive answers. I mentioned to the Brigadier that we had given the Colonel this request. The Brigadier then told me that *he* was the one that would be reporting back - so without ado, he was also given a copy of our questions together with the same request.

There is another point I have just remembered; I cannot remember if it came in the body of the presentation - or in the questions and answer period. It is that several times mention was made not only of the (increasing) importance of other types of soldier - and "high-tech" weaponry, but also of the ability of these other soldiers to very satisfactorily carry out Infantry functions if required. (One non-Infantry corporal in the team was called forward to vouch for the fact that he and others had volunteered for Ulster duties. When Mike asked if they had volunteered a second time he was rapidly "dismissed" and marched back out of sight before he could answer!)

This covers the main items that I recollect of the presentation, and informal "chats" before and after.

Michael has also observed with absolute accuracy and complete justification that, based on the behaviour and apparent attitude of the majority of attendees, the team would be completely within their rights and unchallengeable if they were to report back to the Army Board:

ABERDEEN, pm 7th May:
Presentation took place to audience of about 30.

Slight problem due to the breakdown of a cine projector. Audience received the presentation with little reaction and no adverse comment other than from two apparently well-practiced "trouble makers". However, there should be nothing to fear from them as they received no support whatsoever from the remainder of the audience.

The presentation was introduced by Colonel Clive Fairweather a former Commanding Officer of 1 KOSB. The audience included

Brigadier Frank Coutts and Major Willie Turner from Dumfries. When question time came we asked several pointed questions which Colonel Radcliffe commanding the team, made very little effort to answer.

Frank Coutts wrote to Clive Fairweather the day following in these terms. . .

15th May 1992
Dear Clive,

Since I retired in 1973 I have attended practically every Army Presentation Team visit. That one last night was by far the poorest on record.

OK, the pictures were lovely and an innocent bystander might be taken in by the slick presentation. But it was badly flawed. All the speakers were "below par", churning out their well-worn script parrot-fashion, without any animation, and in some cases they were inaudible, particularly the lassie, who didn't know whether her mike was on or not (my hearing is VG).

Radcliffe got badly fluffed under pressure. Admittedly he had to deal with the KOSB heavy mob - but he dealt with them very inadequately and very unconvincingly. It's simply not good enough for them to take the Jolly Hockey Sticks, "best thing since sliced bread," "everything'll be all right on the night," attitude to Options for Change. They are there to educate but they are also there to sense the mood of the electorate. In that they were most insensitive.

But what really appalled me was the audience - or lack of it. It was a miserably small company, 90% of them home team players. I doubt if there were 10 people there to whom the presentation was really directed. Where was the Lord Lieutenant, the provosts, the headmasters, the career masters, the police, the fire service, the captains of industry, reps from the CBE, the employers - from that impressive bullshit list we see on the screen of firms who support the Army? It was a terrible waste of resources.

Whoever was responsible for assembling that audience let the GOC and you down with a bang and they ought to be told so. It confirms my belief that most officers "just don't want to know" so far as Glasgow and Lanarkshire are concerned.

A poor show. I was going to write to General Peter, but then I thought some of the flak might descend on you - so you can chuck this in the WPB.

Yours Aye,

Frank.

The main body of the audience were obviously servicemen in civvies and one of them a Subaltern came up to us at the end and said "the cuts under Options for Change had not gone far enough, and that the regimental system should be scrapped". The whole presentation was largely a waste of time, and we departed leaving copies of our unanswered questions with Clive Fairweather.

Early in May we heard that the new Defence Secretary was to meet with all Scottish MPs and General MacMillan drafted a letter which Hamish Logan sent to all Scottish MPs as follows...

Lt Col JF Logan
18 Hatton Place
Edinburgh
EH9 1UB

22nd May 1992

All Scottish Members of Parliament

1. General Sir John MacMillan, Chairman of the Keep Our Scottish Battalions Campaign, has asked me to write to you. We understand that all Scottish Members of Parliament are shortly to have a meeting with

the Secretary of State for Defence. Now that we have been promised more open government you, like us, will no doubt expect an explanation of how the government intend to meet the United Kingdom's defence commitments after the cuts in the Armed Forces have been carried out.

2. We are primarily concerned with the cuts proposed in the Infantry where 17 of the current 55 battalions (30.9%) are due to go. The battalion is the 'workhorse' of the Army and even with 55 battalions the frequency of 'emergency tours' usually exceeds the Ministry of Defence's declared target.

For instance: against a target of 24 months between tours of duty in Northern Ireland a number of battalions are returning after only 18 months or less. A Scottish battalion is at present back in Ireland less than 10 months after completing a full emergency tour.

When considering the United Kingdom's contribution to the United Nation's force in Yugoslavia the Ministry of Defence were forced to conclude that no battalion was available.

3. Emergency tours demand a high degree of skill and training which can best be met by Infantry battalions but they also place a considerable strain on all the individuals involved, particularly so on the families. If these tours occur too frequently the quality of life suffers and the wastage rate amongst experienced and well trained men increases.

4. There can be no argument against some cuts at this time particularly where they involve poorly recruited regiments or battalions. However, in our carefully considered collective judgement a cut of 17 battalions when considered against known commitments, let alone the unexpected, is excessive and verging on being irresponsible. We hope that you will question the Secretary of State on this important issue.

5. We are also deeply concerned at the harsh level of cuts to be made in the Scottish Infantry where 3 of our 9 (33%) battalions are due to go.

The recruiting record of the Scottish Division of Infantry is second to none and there can be no doubt that the Division can sustain all the present regiments. Why then has Scotland been singled out for such severe cuts?

6. The Kings Division of Infantry recruiting in the North of England are to lose no battalions. Their recruiting record while good is not as good as the Scottish Division of Infantry. Why the disparity in treatment?

7. We have raised all these issues with the Prime Minister, the previous Secretary of State for Defence as well as with his political and military subordinates without receiving any rational explanation.

8. Figures quoted in Parliament by Mr Winston Churchill in October 1991 put the British contribution to defence in an interesting perspective. For every 1000 of the population countries have the following numbers in their armed forces:

Switzerland	96
Sweden	84
Iraq	52
United States	20
Germany	19
Italy	16
France	15
UK	barely 11

(only Japan amongst the major nations has less.)

Yours sincerely,

Hamish Logan

Lt Col JF Logan

KEEP OUR SCOTTISH BATTALIONS

Chapter 14

King's Own Scottish Borderers
Annual General Meeting Galashiels
16th May 1992

Saturday the 16th May saw the Regimental AGM held in Galashiels attended by Borderers from all over the country and abroad. The Colonel of the Regiment, Brigadier Colin Mattingley, was in the chair, and he read out a message from the Earl of Minto, Convener of Borders Regional Council. . .

Regional Headquarters
Newtown St Boswells
Melrose
TD6 0SA

12th May 1992

My Dear Colonel,

If it becomes appropriate, I should be grateful if you would convey to the Annual General Meeting of the KOSB Association my assurances of the continued and unanimous support of the Borders Regional Council for the future of the Regiment within its separate and singular right. It has been and remains our privilege to have fought for, and to fight for, those, who within the family of the King's Own Scottish Borderers, have given just cause to the unqualified gratitude and pride of every Borderer, over a period of 3 centuries.

I know personally that no opportunity has been missed, by those who have a voice, to draw to the attention of Her Majesty's Government, either directly or indirectly, the considered views of those who value the maintenance of the highest standards within the Armed Forces of the Crown.

On behalf of the Borders Regional Council may I be allowed to congratulate the Regiment upon the high quality of the Campaign.

In wishing you well I trust that the support and the humble endeavours to which I have referred may have been of help.

Good luck to you all.

Yours sincerely

Minto

The 6th Battalion Reunion Club Dinner was also on the 16th May, and as usual was very well attended. Graham Thomson had paid great attention to detail. The Dinner was held in the Kings Hotel, and the Colonel of the Regiment, Brigadier Charles Richardson, and Brigadier Frank Coutts addressed the assembled company. Graham had invited Douglas Robson of the Friends of the Gordon Highlanders to the dinner, and Douglas and I spoke briefly about the Campaign for the regiments. Charlie Laidlaw had told me on the 15th May, that on Sunday the 17th May the *Sunday Times* and the *Sunday Mail* would carry an important announcement regarding ourselves and the Royal Scots. I told the assembled Borderers to buy both papers in the morning. We were aware that journalists from the *Mail* had been in the town on the 16th saying that the regiment had been saved, and taking photographs in the British Legion Club. Sure enough the *Sunday Times* and the *Sunday Mail* carried the story on the 17th May, the *Mail* with a banner front page heading "Fighting Fit". "The KOSB and the Royal Scots are Saved". This was accompanied by photographs of Borderers celebrating in the British Legion Club. Frank Coutts and Douglas Robson who had been staying the night with me read the papers with mixed emotions, and after, some discussion we decided the papers were flying a kite, and that we would only believe it when we had official confirmation. The telephone rang all day with journalists seeking information. Severin Carrell of *The Scotsman* rang to say the MoD were saying they could not confirm the reports, and indeed were denying them. There were calls also from Weeton Barracks, Preston, where the Battalion were based. Mrs Kate White who had been very active in the Campaign and had written letters to Mrs Major and Government Ministers, was particularly disappointed we could not confirm the reports. The reports were denied in *The Scotsman* the following day, and the two Government Ministers quoted as the source for the articles were not identified. This all gave us valuable ammunition to renew our letter writing and pressure on MPs.

On 22nd May, Charlie Laidlaw wrote to me in the following terms. . .

Citigate
17 Ainslie Place
Edinburgh EH3 6AU

22nd May 1992

Dear Donald,
    A short briefing letter to fill you in on (what appears) to be happening - although it is like standing in a hall of mirrors and not quite knowing whether what is going on is reality or distortion.
    It appears that:
    (a) The political case has been well made. The sources for both the *Sunday Times* and *Sunday Mail* were cabinet-level. In a private meeting, Hector Monro confirmed "all was still to play for". (The *Sunday Mail* thought it particularly significant that Rifkind described the *Sunday Times* story as "speculation".)
    (b) The case to officials (whether civilian/military I don't know) has

not yet been accepted. According to Perry Miller, special advisor to Rifkind, and Richard Normington, research desk officer at Tory Central Office, "officials" are still justifying Tom King's original proposals.

The strong advice I have been given, and which I think is good advice, is that:

(a) We need to lever whatever contacts we have at the Ministry of Defence.

(b) We need to reinforce with MPs/Peers that this is a Campaign that won't go away - ie it will remain on the political agenda. To that end, letters to all Scottish MPs are being sent.

We need to try to create dialogue, rather than beat drums. However, if we don't continue that dialogue, the issue will drop off the political agenda - and we will lose.

My own feeling is that we have progressively raised the stakes through this Campaign - our strategy and tactics now have to be thought out and carefully co-ordinated.

I hope this letter provides an outline on events, although I'm more than happy to fill in some of the background.

Best wishes,
Yours sincerely
Charlie
Charles Laidlaw

Chapter 15

The Chairman's Report
and Brigadier Frank Coutts's Report

Following all the excitement of the *Sunday Times* and *Sunday Mail* reports, journalists kept telephoning asking who the two Cabinet Ministers referred to in the reports were. Due to press confidentiality, and the strict rules journalists apply regarding information, we were unable to find out the identity of the Ministers concerned. By listing our known Cabinet "sympathisers" it was not too difficult to hazard an educated guess, that this revelation was a deliberate tactic to highlight the Campaign and the shortcomings of "Options for Change", in an effort to solicit some sort of statement from the Defence Secretary. The tactic was certainly not initiated by the Campaign, and both journalists, and Charlie Laidlaw were adamant it had been initiated by the Ministers concerned. General Sir John MacMillan, due to all the activity and rumour, sent out the following situation report to all campaigners; closely followed by one from Frank Coutts to all Borderers involved in the day to day running of the Campaign. . .

Report from General Sir John MacMillan
28th May 1992.
I have been in touch with a number of the people most involved with the Campaign over recent days, and have agreed that a SITREP is due.
  Since our last meeting the three prongs of the Campaign have been

directed at Parliament, the Press and the MoD.

Several of us have written to Malcolm Rifkind, wishing him well in his appointment, but refraining from pressing our case unduly hard, since he was so well briefed before taking over that such a move could be counterproductive. In his acknowledgement to me, he said that he would find 'the best solution for the Army' - a good political reply!

The MPs have been approached by a number of different people, with the general effect of reminding them of their pledges during the election. In the case of John Home-Robertson, I suggested that he might stir things up again if he was selected to return to the Select Committee, or indeed if he were not that he might remind those who do join the Committee that there is unfinished business to take up. He replied that he very much hoped that he would be on the Committee again, but there seems to be an inordinate delay in this Parliament getting down to business, so we must wait and see on that score. I also approached Hector Monro and asked him to stiffen any resolve that Ian Lang might think of displaying and he agreed to do so. As a result of a report that all the Scottish MPs would be invited to a meeting with Malcolm Rifkind shortly, I asked Sandy Boswell to prepare a briefing note to them all explaining our viewpoint, and that has been despatched to them all at the House of Commons, where they should find it when they return from the present week's recess.

The MoD is where I fear we are not making the headway that I would have liked. Obviously they are giving nothing away, but both as a result of Peter Graham's interview with CGS and intelligence from someone in MO there are people in the MoD who are confident that they can manage on the number of battalions that will remain after the amalgamations and do not place additional battalions high in their priority list if an add-back is on offer. Either they are working with mirrors, or they are all confident that they are either senior enough not to serve with battalions again or intend to leave the Army before the recurrence of NI tours gets them down. Sandy had had quoted to him that the tour intervals will be 29 months "when everything settles down". What has to settle to achieve this is unclear but it must be a force level far less than we have now and absolutely no other commitment such as Yugoslavia. Perhaps the Para will also have to remain acceptable to the Irish Government.

If you hear anything more concrete than rumour on this score it may well give us the occasion to challenge the logic of the MoD.

Finally, the press. The hang-fire while Malcolm Rifkind examines his new responsibilities has given rise to a good deal of speculation which has kept the issue ticking over, but the press has other priorities at present. We must be ready to sieze what openings appear, *but this must be in the same statesmanlike way that we have written throughout the Campaign.* The danger of antagonising potential supporters by being too parochial, and failing to emphasise the bigger Army, and Infantry picture is greater now than it was when there was a good deal of emotion in a subject that was on everybody's lips. By all means introduce new logic, like the greater importance of the ARRC being properly supported by this country as the Franco-German military force takes on any higher profile, or any development in the Balkans which illustrates our powerlessness to pull our weight 'at the heart of Europe', and then point out that we still have the strongest Division and could help if we were allowed to. *But make sure that any comment is firm and to the point, and doesn't get confused with too many words.* (This letter runs that risk.)

Finally, there has been some suggestion that we should hold another meeting. I would be happy to do so if I could see any useful agenda, and if any of you feel that there is meat to discuss, and would like to table any paper, then we could convene a meeting. I am extremely busy and would resent the time if there was nothing to discuss, and I wouldn't want a lot of people to travel long distances for no purpose, but, as I said before, I would appear if someone has business that needs a meeting. Don't hesitate to get on to the telephone if you would like to discuss this. Meanwhile, keep gently nudging the case along, and make use of any openings that invite a balanced comment challenging the MoD's desire for expensive toys in place of real soldiers.

Frank Coutts' report made three main points:

1. That we should not hassle Malcolm Rifkind as the case for our retention has been clearly made. We should give him time.

2. That it was unlikely we would have a statement from him until the House of Commons reassembles in the Autumn.

3. There are definite indications that any Infantry add-back would include the cancellation of the RS/KOSB amalgamation.

Frank went on to say that the unusually high rate of acceptance of our letters to Editors was evidence of the support for our cause, by both the media and the general public. Our Campaign banner had been prominently displayed at all the Border Common Ridings and telemessages of support had been sent to all Stand-ard Bearers, Cornets etc from Operation Borderer. He went on to say he had talked with Lord James Douglas-Hamilton and Sir Hector Monro of the Scottish Office, also with General Sir Peter Graham GOC Scotland and with General Sir John MacMillan our Campaign Chairman. Frank also pointed out that a great deal of paper was flying about to try and summarise it all would only confuse. He urged us to keep making the points and arguments put by General MacMillan in his report to all cam-paigners.

The next event that had a major bearing on the momentum of the Campaign was the annual Minden Day Parade at Glencorse Barracks, which was being combined with the Korean reunion to mark the 50th anniversary. RHQ had been working on this reunion for some months, and Borderers attended from all over the world, including Willie Purves, the Chairman of the Hong Kong and Shanghai Bank, who, as a National Service Subultern, had won the DSO in Korea. We asked him if he would attend and speak at our forthcoming Rally, but as he was to return to Hong

Kong on the day of the Rally, he had to decline. The gathering of so many Borderers was extremely useful in gaining support for our Rally, and spreading the latest news from Operation Borderer. The Korean Veterans were at Glencorse for the weekend, for a dinner and church parade, but some of us travelled through by bus for the parade on Saturday the 1st August, returning some two hours late, having been held up by some of the 4th Bn who got lost in the Sgts Mess, much to the irritation of Graham Thomson who told them so on the bus. He accused them of being late for the bus, and late for the war, which provoked quite a discussion! To make matters worse only 3 miles from Glencorse they wanted to stop for fish and chips. Graham was furious and although he was starving refused to accept the offer of a chip from any of the 4th Bn.

Chapter 16

Galashiels Rally
22nd August 1992

After much discussion regarding the Rally on August 22nd, Graham Thomson and I agreed that we needed to get a well known speaker so we decided to try and get General Norman Schwartzkopf who had commanded the allied troops in the Gulf War with such success. I wrote to the American Embassy in London, who replied that the General could be contacted at MacDili Air Force Base in Florida, c/o General Command. The following letter was dispatched inviting the General to speak at our Rally. . .

22nd June 1992

Dear General,

You may be aware of the Campaign to "Keep Our Scottish Battalions" in the face of government proposals to amalgamate four of our most famous regiments; the Royal Scots with the King's Own Scottish Borderers and the Queens Own Highlanders with the Gordon Highlanders. This proposal has caused outrage in Scotland as the aforementioned regiments have 1,200 years of outstanding service between them.

The All Party Defence Committee in their report in March were extremely critical of the proposals, and have asked the government to think again. Our Campaign presented a petition of a million signatures to Parliament, which we raised in six weeks.

Informed government sources indicate the new Defence Minister, Malcolm Rifkind, is planning an add-back of at least four battalions, and that our Campaign's arguments based on military requirements rather than sentiment are having the desired effect.

We plan a mass Rally in the heart of our regimental country in late summer. You, Sir, command international respect following the Gulf War, especially with the Scottish Division, and we wondered if you would consider being our main speaker at the Rally? It goes without saying we would pay all expenses. The proposed date of the Rally is 22nd August... but this can be changed to suit your availability. General Sir John MacMillan, our Campaign Chairman and several prominent politicians would speak in support.

We are so near to winning our battle we feel, Sir, your presence would help to "tip the scales". Perhaps when we have your reaction we can get down to firm planning re date, travel arrangements etc. Please give us your earnest consideration.

Yours respectfully

W Donald Fairgrieve

Operation Borderer

NEMO ME IMPUNE LACESSIT

After two weeks had elapsed I became impatient, and telephoned MacDili Air Base and asked for the Duty Officer. The Duty Officer confirmed that my letter had arrived but would not give me the General's telephone number, as he was no longer a serving officer. He suggested I telephone the Defence Department, who put me on to the Public Affairs Office in the White House. I had a long conversation with a Secretary who agreed to contact General Schwarzkopf and find out it he could come. Some days later we received a very nice letter from him regretting he could not attend due to prior commitments, but wishing us all the best in our Campaign. We had made public the fact that we had invited "Stormin Norman" to the Rally and got valuable publicity for the Rally as a result.

John Home-Robertson, a member of the Select Committee on Defence, had again agreed to speak at the Rally, as had Sir David Steel MP and Archie Kirkwood MP. We were having great difficulty in finding a Conservative MP to speak, Winston Churchill MP and Sir Nicholas Fairbairn QC MP both replied saying they had prior engagements. Approaches to General Sir Anthony Farrar-Hockley and General Sir Martin Frandale proved unsuccessful, but solicited letters of support. We had been aware of the very high profile Campaign being waged by the Staffords in the south, led by Brigadier Levey who was due to attend our Keep Our Scottish Battalions meeting in Edinburgh on 21st August. We also knew that Brigadier Levey was friendly with Allan Alstead who although having to keep a low profile because of his job as Chief Executive of the Sports Council, was still very active in the Campaign. John Levey and the Staffords had used Westminster Communications as lobbyists at Westminster, as we had through Citigate, and we resolved to ask him to address the Rally. He accepted willingly, as he was to be in Edinburgh for the meeting the day before the Rally. We were determined to find a Conservative to complete the platform party, as we had always presented a cross party image, and several telephone calls were made to Conservative Central Office, without success. We knew that Christine Richard, the leader of the Edinburgh Conservative Group on the City Council was supportive, and in fact had stood as a Conservative Candidate in the Borders, and so invited her to speak. She accepted, and we set about emphasising to the press her connection with Edinburgh and the KOSB as the Edinburgh Regiment.

Pipe Major David Bunyan had assembled a formidable pipe band made up of Peebles, Innerleithen, Stow, Langholm, Annan and Galashiels pipe bands, and we invited Selkirk Silver Band,

101

and a combination of Galashiels and St Boswells town bands to take part in the Rally. I had written to Colonel Mike Ashmore asking the Royal Scots to support the Rally, and he replied saying they would bring a coach load of Royal Scots from Edinburgh. The Gordons had agreed to bring a party down, and Willie Turner was encouraging Borderers in Dumfries and Galloway to attend. The Colonel of the Regiment had agreed to speak, although Frank Coutts was unable to attend due to a charity fair he was organising in Edinburgh. This was a disappointment as Frank had done so much to galvanise public support in his speech the year previously, at our first Rally. Although not present, Frank marched up and down at his charity fair playing the pipes at the time the Rally was taking place and helped to raise £27,000 for Trefoil funds.

Charlie Laidlaw came down to Galashiels following the Keep Our Scottish Battalions meeting in Edinburgh, on Friday 21st August, to set up a press point. John Levey of the Staffords had reported to the meeting the progress we had made at Westminster, and the situation as he saw it. We had a great deal of support amongst MPs he reported, but the Ministry of Defence were still sticking to Tom King's original plans, although a softening of attitude could be detected in the Minister's statements and letters. Douglas Robson and Willie Turner accompanied me to Galashiels where we were joined by Mrs Kate White and her husband Sgt Jim White who had come up from 1 KOSB at Weeton. They reported that there would be very few attending the Rally from Weeton, because of duties, and the delicate situation of serving soldiers being seen on what was a protest march. When I arrived in the Burgh Yard (Rally assembly point) on the morning of the 22nd, I was amazed at the turn out. Pipe Major David Bunyan was tuning up his massed band, Legion Colour Parties were assembling, and a huge number of Borderers were already congregating. They were soon to be joined by two coach loads from Edinburgh containing the Royal Scots, and the

Edinburgh KOSB Association members. The Gordon Highlanders contingent who had arrived the night before, and had only had a few hours sleep, and had brought grins to the faces of the town's publicans, were organising their banners. There was a real atmosphere of "Wha daur meddle wi us" about. Douglas Robson had already been interviewed by one of the many television crews, and the press point (a borrowed caravan) was busy with journalists.

General Sir John MacMillan had been asked to lay a wreath at the War Memorial at 10.00 am to draw the media to the start of the Rally. He laid the wreath and was interviewed by national television and radio, while Major Ken Fraser and Graham Thomson tried to get the Parade into some semblance of order. We had invited all the Border Provosts, Border Principals (Cornets, Standard Bearers, Braw Lads etc) and Border Rugby Clubs to take part, and as many of them had no military background Ken Fraser and Graham Thomson had no easy task. The Parade stepped off at 10.30 led by General Sir John MacMillan, Sir David Steel MP, John Home-Robertson MP, Brigadier John Levey and Christine Richard, behind the massed pipe bands. They were followed by ex-Borderers, ex-servicemen and women, Royal British Legion Colour Parties, Border provosts and principles. The rear was brought up by the Selkirk Silver Band, playing the Border tunes and also followed by the public. On arrival at the Scott park in the centre of Galashiels, the Rally was addressed by the speakers, all of whom were very critical of Options for Change, and the Ministry of Defence. John Home-Robertson in particular blasted the Government and the Ministry of Defence who, in a letter, had stated that the Select Committee on Defence had broadly agreed with the proposals made by Tom King. He described the letter as "damned impertinence", and the Ministry of Defence of being "economical with the truth". The Rally attended by over 3,000, was a great success being reported on the national television news on both channels and the BBC overseas service.

Immediately following the Rally we laid on a lunch for VIPs and the press in the TA Officers Mess in Galashiels. This was a most useful exercise as our speakers and the press were able to mingle and exchange views. Jim Cockburn, a local butcher whose father had served in the regiment, donated the meat for the meal, prepared by my wife Pat and her helpers. Graham Thomson had purchased wine with what was left of our fast diminishing Operation Borderer funds, but had not thought to provide a corkscrew which proved to be an embarrassment as the VIPs arrived prior to most of us who were still engaged in the Beer Tent at the Scott Park. John Home-Robertson MP came to Pat's rescue by producing a corkscrew and, opening bottles, remarked that it was standard equipment for a Border farmer!

We were greatly encouraged by the support from all sections of the community, and went to bed planning another Rally in Edinburgh during the European Conference, and a lobby of the Conservative Party Conference in Brighton during the Parliamentary recess. General Sir John MacMillan wrote to me after the Rally in the following terms. . .

23rd August 1992

Dear Donald,

That was a splendid day on Saturday. You really achieved quite the best response you could have expected, despite the threat of rain, and the politicians did you proud. It is very good to hear them all speaking with one voice, even if they all have the advantage that they are not in a position to have to find the money to pay for the extra battalions. I had a good chat with both David Steel and John Home-Robertson on the way back to the TA Centre, and I am sure that the latter will do all he can to continue the fight in the Select Committee.

I missed the report on the Scottish news that night, but understand one of the interviews I had with a BBC correspondent made the World News, and my son-in-law heard it in Zimbabwe!

Well done indeed.

Yours

John

During the weekend of the Galashiels Rally, Willie Turner and I had the opportunity to discuss with Charlie Laidlaw the idea of a Rally in Edinburgh. This we discussed well into the night and the following morning. Charlie wrote to all sections of the Campaign on 25th August in the following terms. . .

Citigate,
25th August 1992

Following our conversation this morning, the germ of the idea for the heads of government summit in Edinburgh is:

We hand in to the President of the EC (ie John Major) a 'petition' from the people of Scotland, as represented by their elected district and regional councils. The petition would have the signature of each provost. It could physically be handed in by Provost Irons, representing the host city on behalf of his fellow Provosts. The police would have no objection to an event of this nature.

Depending on how the police react to staging an event around the petition, we could, for example:

* invite a gaggle of provosts (as many as can come)
* have representatives of the committee present
* have representatives from each regiment present
* have contingents from each regiment present
* have a full-blown march/rally somewhere in Edinburgh

Realistically, if we don't detect a softening of the MoD line soon, we will have to raise the stakes. In other words, raise the political temperature and force Rifkind to re-think - whatever his MoD advisors say. This we can best do directly to the Prime Minister at a time when he will have other things to think about - at a venue where he desperately wants everything to run smoothly. The beauty of this idea is that, depending on what happens between now and then, we can make it as low-key or high-key as we choose.

Can you let me know what you think? My obvious concern is to set the wheels in motion - otherwise we run the risk of not getting the provosts' signatures. I am mindful that the 'petition' will need careful drafting; I can take specific advice on this.

I'm sorry that the idea has perminated so soon after the last committee meeting when it could have been debated fully. I'll be on holiday until Thursday 3rd September, although still contactable *in extremis*.

Yours sincerely

Charlie Laidlaw

At the beginning of September Mike Ashmore produced a paper entitled "Save the Royal Scots - Where are we now?" This paper which Mike has kindly allowed me to reproduce did much to unite all the efforts of the various Regimental pressure groups, and point the way forward during the Parliamentary recess.

Chapter 17

"Save The Royal Scots"

Paper by Colonel Mike Ashmore OBE
Save The Royal Scots - Where are we now?

Introduction

1. After a year of our Campaign to save the regiment I thought it would be helpful to set down the situation as we stand now and to suggest some action for the future. I hope that you will add to the paper with your own ideas and suggestions. My main aim is to provoke discussion. This discussion to be focused around the time of the Regimental Cocktail Party and in particular at a meeting to be held in RHQ on Friday 11 September at 1400 hrs. Parliament reassembles in mid October so we must have our plans laid.

What have we achieved?

2. The Keep Our Scottish Battalions Campaign, of which we are an integral part, have achieved a great deal namely:

   a. The petition signed by 1,000,000 people.

   b. We have the support of the public in Scotland without a doubt. To the extent that people elsewhere care about us then we also have their support.

   c. We have the support of a considerable number of media people at both local and national level.

d. A large majority of Scottish MPs of all political persuasions have pledged their support.

e. Local Government, particularly within the regimental areas of the afflicted regiments, are solidly behind us.

f. Certain distinguished members of the House of Lords have spoken in our favour.

g. The Commons Select Committee came out strongly in our favour. Furthermore the new committee will return to the subject in October.

3. The Campaign in Scotland has presented a united front and so one of our greatest achievements has been to prevent the MoD from creating divisions in our ranks.

4. A measure of how deeply offended people are by the proposals in Options for Change was the turnout by Royal Scots and KOSBs in Galashiels last weekend.

Who are our friends and what can we ask them to do to help us?
5. This list is not comprehensive and hopefully you will be able to add to it:

a. The Royal family have made their displeasure known. Can we ask our Colonel in Chief to do any more?

b. Within the House of Lords, Lords Swinfen and Wedgwood have lost no opportunity. Lords Brammall and Chalfont have spoken strongly against Options for Change. Lord Vivian has joined the fray. Should we now approach Lady Thatcher, Lords Whitelaw, Owen and others? Lord Chalfont has a question on the subject due to come up in October.

c. In the House of Commons John Home-Robertson is our staunchiest ally closely followed by other members of the Select Committee. Michael Mates and Hector Monro are now Ministers but both have strongly supported our case in the past.

d. Amongst the media we have received support from:
The Daily Telegraph - John Keegan and Allan Massie

The Sunday Times
The Times - Michael Evans and Christy Campbell
Scotland on Sunday - Trevor Royle
The Herald - Ian Bruce
The Scotsman - Severin Carrell
The Edinburgh Evening News - David Thompson
The Daily Record - Alan Gulland
Perhaps we should be writing formally to editors again.

Who are our opponents?

6. The government have maintained their original stance against all the arguments. They have done so by carefully avoiding public recognition of the Campaign, treating every approach as being from an individual. They have managed skillfully to misrepresent the facts. They have studiously avoided answering specific questions, trotting out the same half truths in all their replies. When pressed they have resorted to making statements expressing "hope that tour intervals will return to normal" or "full manning will solve the problem".

7. The Army Board have not taken up our case even though it is in the long term interests of the Army. We have to ask why?

a. Is it because they believe the politicians will restore the Infantry numbers whatever and so they can concentrate their efforts on lesser priorities and thus hope to achieve both?

b. Do they genuinely believe that "Options for Change" has got it right?

c. Are they primarily concerned with cash limits?

d. Are they afraid to lose face?

8. There exist also two further threats, not yet publicly identified to any great extent.

a. Postpone individual amalgamations to meet immediate commitments in the hope that peace will break out in NI or Sarajevo.

b. Encourage a change to a system of large regiments.

Both of these would be disastrous to our case, except that the first would so adversely affect morale as well as causing enormous administrative difficulties that it is hard to believe even the present Army Board would sign up to it. The second option might be welcome if only because it would bring back into the argument the rest of the Scottish regiments, the Household Brigade and the English regiments who so far have escaped the axe to such an extent that "Options" might have to be reopened.

Some conclusions from the foregoing

9. The extent of our support is so widespread and so strong that we have to ask why we have so far failed to make any apparent impact on the government. I say apparent for there have been persistent rumours to the effect that the RS/KOSB amalgamation will be stopped etc. While such rumours are welcome and give encouragement we cannot allow ourselves to sit back and wait for it to happen. The lack of any helpful response from the government is born of:

a. Cabinet collective responsibility for Tom King.

b. Allowance of a decent interval since the election for Malcolm Rifkind to find a face saving formula.

c. Concern about financial implications at a time of tight restrictions on public spending.

d. Pre-occupation with the economy to the detriment of Foreign and Defence policy, both of which seem to be rooted in the last 40 years and not geared to the future.

The Campaign in the next six months

10. Our arguments have been developed at three separate levels.

a. Sentiment - This has been an appeal by the regiments on historical and social grounds. This may carry no weight with Ministers but it is constituency MPs at the end of the day who vote in Parliament and they are influenced by public opinion. We must therefore continue to do what we can at this level.

b. The Military Case - This has been the central theme to the

Campaign. The argument is for the Infantry as a whole; for sufficient numbers to meet existing commitments. In the last 12 months the situation has deteriorated in that NI has an additional long term commitment of one Infantry battalion and Bosnia seems certain to require another. How long this latter will last is hard to say but it will surely be some years. We do not gloat about this but instead point out that this merely illustrates what we have been saying all along.

c. Foreign and Defence Policy - The most recent Defence white paper has yet to be debated in Parliament. It is wide open to attack:

1) It relates more to the Cold War than to the present day.

Emphasis on Nuclear weapons High-tech equipment at the expense of manpower Manpower levels related to specific commitments.

2) Little evident connection between what the Foreign Office desire and what MoD will provide. Is our lack of response to the UN due to lack of resources?

3) The so called Rapid Reaction Corps is anything but rapid. 20 days has been quoted as the minimum warning period for the battalion earmarked for Bosnia. That combined with the shilly-shallying of the politicians makes the deployment of the BEF to France in 1914 look like a miracle.

4) There appears to be no intention to deploy Peace keeping forces unless absolutely forced to do so. Much has been made of our current contributions with the implication that we have done our bit.

These arguments lead to a call for a proper review of Defence. Not an in house exercise in cutting costs but a proper public debate involving the RUSI, ISS, Academics etc from without the MoD. There is considerable support for such a review but the Labour Party are as bankrupt over Defence as the present government so there has been no-one to articulate these ideas.

Agenda for Action

11. Local/Sentiment level

Lobbying of Heads of Government in Edinburgh in December (See attached proposal from Citigate)

Letters to local papers
Stories from 1st Battalion in local papers
Press and TV coverage of Regimental Events

12. The Military Case
Lobby of Commons Select Committee
Questions in Parliament
Letters to the National papers
Letters to leading figures, Thatcher, Owen etc
Letters to Ministers
Articles in the press

13. The Strategic level
As for 12 above but with emphasis on the wider aspects of Defence
Policy.
Please let me have your comments, suggestions etc. Phone me at
home (0899) 20473, or catch me at the Cocktail Party, or come to the
meeting on Friday 11 September at 1400 hrs in RHQ
Mike Ashmore

Frank Coutts wrote to Mike Ashmore after reading his report...

11th September 1992

Dear Mike,
Donald very kindly sent me a copy of your excellent paper "Where
are we now?"
You have hit so many nails on the head that I could hear the clank
all the way from Cocklaw. Bravo.
We shall now be conferring regimentally to plan The Way Ahead. It
will be interesting to hear the outcome of your deliberations today.
My view is that we should press on three-pronged:
1. Massive demo (but dignified) for EEC visit in December.
2. Lean heavily on Defence Select Committee and All Party Defence

Group.

3. Continue letters to press as opportunity arises. I suspect there will be no lack of opportunity. Donald suspects that the economy may now be the excuse - but the government has never given two hoots for defence money required viz WWI & II, Falklands, Gulf etc. Change priorities, drop a Trident or two.

Thank you for your guidance. Keep up the good work.

Yours ever,

Frank C

Campaign Organiser Charlie Laidlaw wrote to General Sir John MacMillan on 9th September in the following terms which also served to narrow down our field of attack and present a united front. . .

Citigate 9th September 1992

Dear John,

I thought I should write following the last committee meeting, and having spoken informally to Donald Fairgrieve, Mike Robson and Mike Ashmore since then. I note also that John Levey is meeting Christy Campbell of *The Sunday Telegraph*, and the further informal representations have been made by Westminster Communications to members of the Committee. No doubt it is a subject to which we will return. Incidentally, Simon Nayyar is again meeting Malcolm Rifkind's special advisor next week to determine how far he has "gone native" - something which I guess has to be our overriding concern in view of the advice he is likely to be receiving from CGS.

The current problem, as I see it, is that we appear to have won the political argument, but failed to win military support. (Other priorities appear to be uppermost, given CGS's comments at that recent briefing). Our task would therefore appear to be to:

(a) maintain political pressure, primarily through the Defence Select Committee.

(b) make the military case whenever we can, and ensure that Ministers are aware of the MoD's concern over Infantry (which may be at variance with what Rifkind is being told).

(c) maintain the Campaign in Scotland; to provide a focus for public concern, and so reinforce political pressure at the local level.

Whilst (a) will primarily mean briefing the Defence Select Committee (and contacts have already been made) it may also mean a presence at, at least, the Tory conference. I'd be glad to hear your views. My own feeling is that the situation in Bosnia is still too volatile; any lobbying at the Tory conference must enable us to maintain the moral high ground - rather than open us to any accusation of gloating over misfortune. A couple of newspapers have already suggested that the situation in the former Yugoslavia has given us new hope.

The second aim (b) is less easy, particularly as far as the press and media are concerned. We have made the case repeatedly and it is difficult to see how we can go on making it without there being new developments. I am, however, greatly concerned that the advice Rifkind may be receiving is at variance to acknowledged need; in other words, CGS says we will be five Infantry battalions short, yet he won't be asking for them.

Our aim in (c) is more obvious: to ensure that the Campaign is seen to be continuing in Scotland and that both Scottish cabinet ministers are aware of it. I am mindful that we don't want (indeed, could not) return to the high-profile days of last summer. Rather, we need to keep the Campaign on the local political agenda by ensuring that our presence is seen as well as our voice is heard. One idea that I think has merit is to organise a round-robin petition signed by each Provost or convenor in the Scottish district and regional councils, calling on the government to recognise the case for the Infantry. I've taken soundings from the KOSBs, Gordons and Royal Scots who are in favour. I'd be glad of your view, as I'd like to begin the drafting process and put the wheels in motion. (I should add that no additional costs are involved!)

Donald Fairgrieve and I are meeting with Lothian and Borders Police in the near future to determine what kind of an event could be staged around the time of the heads of government summit in Edinburgh in early December. In discussions I have had with them, the police are both supportive and co-operative; however, I will let you know what our options are once that meeting has taken place.

I hope the above is helpful and I look forward to hearing from you.

Yours sincerely

Charlie

Chapter 18

The Visit of the Scottish Secretary
to Borders Regional Council
3rd September 1992

It was announced that the Scottish Secretary Ian Lang was to visit Borders Regional Council on the 3rd September at their offices in Newtown St Boswells. We organised a party of Borderers including Frank and Morag Coutts to assemble at St Boswells, where we surrounded the entrance to the Council Offices. We had the Keep Our Scottish Battalions banner and the Save the KOSB banner prominently displayed for Ian Lang's arrival. When his car arrived, Graham Thomson and I stepped forward and handed him a letter. He asked who we were and replied "Oh, *you* are Donald Fairgrieve," and accepted the letter. He then crossed the road and spoke to Frank Coutts and the other Borderers. We were lucky that television crews were filming his arrival, and again got prime news coverage. We fell out to the Station Hotel where we enjoyed several refreshments to celebrate another media coup for Operation Borderer.

Letter to Rt Hon Ian Lang MO Secretary of State for Scotland (handed to him during visit to Borders Region).

3rd September 1992
Dear Mr Lang,
Operation Borderer wish to again draw your attention to the serious situation brought about by government proposals under

"Options for Change".

Our Infantry battalions are suffering extreme overstretch before the amalgamations in the Scottish Division are implemented. This is clearly illustrated by regiments having to return to Northern Ireland after only ten months, and our inability to meet our commitments in Europe.

The regiments of the Scottish Division are a special case, as they are part of the fabric of life in Scotland, and are fully recruited and have a good retention record. They have been treated disgracefully as pointed out by the Select Committee on Defence.

Please use your influence with the Minister of Defence to look at the proposals again, in light of world events. John Home-Robertson MP, a member of the Select Committee said on 22nd August at a Rally in Galashiels, attended by thousands of Borderers, "The government is playing fast and loose with regiments which have a vital role in National and International security in a viciously unstable world".

Please urge the government to think again.

Yours sincerely,

W Donald Fairgrieve

All through the summer and much of the previous autumn, Douglas Robson and I had carried on a lengthy correspondence with the Assistant Secretary to the Minister of Defence, a Mr JB Stainton. It was Mr Stainton's letter to us that John Home-Robertson referred to as "damned impertinence" when he stated that the Select Committee agreed broadly with "Options for Change". Mr Stainton in his replies to us, had always maintained that a 2 year gap between emergency tours was achievable "after restructuring". It had been obvious to us that this was impossible, and in fact had never been achieved since the Falklands War. It was clear that the best gap they could achieve was 18 months, and in some cases 15 months and this was before the amalgamations took place. Douglas and I did all we could to get the Ministry of Defence to repeat this claim of 24 months as often as possible, as we knew it was nonsense, and sooner or later they would have to admit it. The other reason for not achieving the target gap between tours that Mr Stainton kept repeating to us was the "unavailability of regiments due to preparing for amalgamation". We knew this was untrue as 6 of the regiments due for amalgamation were either on active service or training for an emergency tour. We were able to expose this early the following January.

The Select Committee on Defence were summoned to a meeting on 22nd September at which Mr Archie Hamilton, Minister of State for the Armed Forces, admitted that intervals between tours to Ulster were likely to be between 15 and 19 months. This was a considerable climb down from his position a year earlier when he wrote to Douglas Robson saying, "It is plainly wrong to assert that the future Army is bound to be overstretched and to declare - as you did in your letter to the press (*Daily Mail*) - that units will have to go to Northern Ireland twice in every 30 months. Such unjustified prognosis of pain and grief increased the concerns of personnel and their families who are already affected by the uncertainties which attend restructuring." This was the breakthrough we had been working for, and we were further heartened to hear from General Sir John MacMillan that he had been invited to attend a meeting with Sir Nicholas Bonsor, the new Chairman of the Select Committee. General Sir John wrote to us as follows. . .

22nd September 1992
To All Regimental Reps and KOSB Campaigners.

I have been invited to attend a meeting with Sir Nicholas Bonsor, the new Chairman of the House of Commons Select Committee on Defence on 12th October, when he will be preparing the questions to put to the Ministry of Defence about the Options package.

I will need every bit of up to date information I can get hold of before I see him. If you have any information on the following it would be invaluable:

Emergency tour intervals now affecting your own battalions or others.

Scale of applications for redundancy particularly among NCOs.

Instances of potential officer or soldier recruits who have decided not to join their local regiments because of the uncertain future in an amalgamated regiments.

Any increase in PVR (premature voluntary retirement) or acceptance of notice point related to forthcoming amalgamations.

The occasions over the four years when restrictions have been placed on adult or junior recruiting. (This is particularly important to counter the argument that we could not sustain that full number of battalions in the Division).

Problems anticipated by local authorities in finding housing or job vacancies for redundant soldiers. Philip Halford-McLeod may be able to help here.

Anything else you feel may be relevant, particularly in the light of the response by the MoD to the previous Committee.

I must have your ideas by 5th October if I am to prepare a good brief, and earlier if possible.

Yours ever

John

All the letter writing by Douglas Robson and myself to the southern press during the summer was beginning to have an effect. We noticed phrases and facts and figures we had used in our letters appearing in editorials in the southern press. Even the *Daily Telegraph* repeated an argument put forward by Douglas in a letter which they had seen fit not to publish. We were talking frequently to southern based journalists, who by now had our telephone numbers. Charlie Laidlaw, himself an ex-journalist, was very helpful in this, as he encouraged journalists to telephone us to check regimental facts. Because of the delicate situation serving soldiers were in, we did our best not to involve them, especially on matters such as the effect on morale of redundancies and the supply of manpower to undermanned southern regiments, for emergency tours. We worked for some weeks on a story for Paul Keel of the *Sunday Mail*, only to abort it at the last minute at the request of the Battalion Commander. It must be said that the Army despite all the uncertainty about their future, carried on in a most professional manner, content to let the campaigners get on with the arguments. This was a point made by General Sir John MacMillan when he met with Malcolm Rifkind in December following the Edinburgh Rally, and the European Summit in Edinburgh.

Chapter 19

The Edinburgh Rally
11th December 1992

On the 15th October, we held a meeting in the Isle of Skye Hotel in Perth attended by Mike and Douglas Robson (Gordons), Malcolm Gomme-Duncan (Black Watch), Willie Turner, Graham Thomson and myself (KOSB) chaired by Charlie Laidlaw. We further discussed the possibility of a Rally in Edinburgh to coincide with the European Summit Conference. We decided it was too good an opportunity to miss and decided to hold it on the 11th December at 10.45, assembling at Kings Stables Road, and marching through Princes Street Gardens to the Ross Band Stand. It was decided to present a petition signed by all local authorities in Scotland to the Prime Minister. We also discussed the possibility of approaching Scottish businesses to sponsor the Rally. Following the meeting Charlie Laidlaw had arranged a meeting with Severin Carrell of *The Scotsman* in the offices of Citigate in Edinburgh. We had a most useful discussion with him, and updated him with General Sir John's meeting with Sir Nicholas Bonsor, and the Campaign in general. On the 21st October, we called a meeting of Borderers in Galashiels to drum up support for the Edinburgh Rally. This was very well attended.

Arrangements were made for the distribution of posters advertising the Rally and the booking of transport to take people to Edinburgh. It was also decided to approach Alloa Brewery to sponsor the Rally as all our meetings were held in the Salmon Inn which is an Alloa inn. The Keep Our Scottish Battalions Committee met in the Royal Scot Club in Edinburgh on the 29th October. General MacMillan welcomed those attending and outlined the two main subjects on the agenda.

a. Evidence to be given to the Commons Select Committee on Defence.

b. The arrangements for the Rally in Edinburgh on the 11th December.

General MacMillan reported that Sir Nicholas Fairbairn MP would lead a delegation to Mr Rifkind, Defence Minister, consisting of John Home-Robertson MP, Menzies Campbell MP and Andrew Welsh MP. General MacMillan would also attend. A sub-committee to deal with the Rally was set up under the chairmanship of Colonel Mike Ashmore, the members appointed were Charlie Laidlaw, Major Campbell Graham, General Young and myself.

Campbell Graham, known as "the voice" is the Scots Guards rep on the main committee and the manager of the Lady Haig's Poppy Factory. As befitting an ex-regimental Sgt-Major there was never any difficulty in hearing what he had to say. He was to be a trump card in organising the huge turnout of ex-servicemen at the Edinburgh Rally.

It was also agreed to form a Glasgow committee under the chairmanship of Major Taylor. The sub-committees were to examine ways of publicising the Rally including leafletting particularly in Edinburgh, announcements nationally and locally on television and radio, and by letters to the press. Mike Ashmore drafted a letter to be sent out to Scottish businesses which is reproduced here. . .

In July 1991 Mr Tom King, then the Secretary of State for Defence, announced the reductions in our Armed Forces under the title 'Options for Change'. These reductions were seen as being possible following the collapse of the threat from the Warsaw Pact. Included in these reductions were the proposed amalgamation of four Scottish Infantry Battalions and the disbandment of another.

Since the end of the Second World War the Infantry have borne the brunt of the operational task faced by the British Army; Malaya, Kenya, Cyprus, Borneo, Aden and more recently Northern Ireland. To meet these commitments it has been essential to have sufficient Infantry to allow for a reasonable gap between operational tours. Failure to do so results in a loss of morale and poor retention in the service of highly skilled personnel. At the same time proper training of units for their primary role suffers. The Ministry of Defence have long recognised this and have set a target interval of 24 months between operational tours, each of which last six months.

The decision to reduce the Scottish Battalions gave rise to a considerable protest. First, because some famous names were to disappear, but also because Scotland was seen to be taking an unfair share of the cuts, particularly as the Scottish Infantry have an excellent record in terms of recruiting when compared with some other regiments which are to survive. More important, however was the realisation that with the proposed number of battalions (38) it would never be possible to achieve the planned interval of 24 months between tours. So the Campaign to save the Scottish Battalions was launched. In October 1991 a petition, signed by 1,000,000 people was handed to Parliament.

In the intervening months the campaigners have maintained the pressure on the government by lobbying in Parliament, by articles and letters in the major national newspapers, by briefing the Commons Select Committee on Defence and by the occasional public demonstration of support for the Campaign. After the General Election and the appointment of Malcolm Rifkind as Secretary of State for Defence the decision was made to allow time for him to settle into his new appointment. Recently Mr Rifkind has said that he would be prepared to reconsider the decisions taken under 'Options for Change' if at any time new commitments arise. In the past year an additional battalion has been sent to Northern Ireland and another is deploying to Bosnia.

The Ministry of Defence have now admitted that the tour interval is 15 months. It has also become apparent that more and more we are likely to be required to provide peace keeping forces in support of the UN, a task most suited to the Infantry.

We believe the time has come for the government to review its decisions. First, because regiments are already being run down to prepare for amalgamation, but secondly and more importantly because morale amongst the Infantry is beginning to suffer. Applications for redundancy far exceed the number of vacancies and concern is being expressed about the future. There is a growing lack of faith in Whitehall.

On 11th December, during the European Summit in Edinburgh, the Campaign will stage a march in Princes Street Gardens to demonstrate to the Prime Minister the depth of feeling which exists in Scotland in support of the Campaign. At the same time we shall be handing to the Prime Minister a declaration of support passed by all the regional and district councils. To make the march a success we plan to bring people from all over Scotland. We have plenty of volunteers but we need help to meet the costs of transport etc. We already have the support of a number of firms, but my purpose in writing is to ask for your support. We believe this is an important cause, not only for Scotland but for the Nation as a whole. If it would suit you to give such support in the form of sponsorship then that can be arranged and due recognition of your contribution would be made.

I would be most grateful if you would reply to me:-

Colonel MBH Ashmore CBE c/o RHQ The Royal Scots (The Royal Regiment) The Castle EDINBURGH EH1 2YT

Yours sincerely

MBH Ashmore

I had received a letter from John MacKenzie, the managing director of Alloa Brewery, who although saying they had a policy of not supporting "political" initiatives, they were anxious to help providing a number of other companies took part. United

124

Distillers through the help of Dr Alan Rutherford also agreed to help and Bells Islander Whisky was added to our generous sponsors. This sponsorship was essential as it enabled us to transport supporters from all over Scotland, and in addition, guaranteed us a good party after the Rally. Charlie Laidlaw set about writing to every local authority in Scotland asking them to sign the declaration we were to present to the Prime Minister on the 11th December, which was as follows. . .

A Declaration from Scottish District and Regional Councils to the Prime Minister

Scotland has always taken pride in the achievements of its sons who have left home to build a new life in a wider service. Their names are recorded on maps throughout the world. That pride is now enshrined in our Scottish Infantry Regiments. They still perform the same selfless tasks; and they still carry the spirit of our pioneering ancestors to the danger spots of a troubled world.

They are now threatened, not by the Queen's enemies, but by Her Majesty's Government. Despite their proven ability to recruit and retain more soldiers than any Division drawn from other parts of the United Kingdom, our regiments are being forced into amalgamation.

This gives us grave cause for concern. Our local economies are suffering, unemployment is a serious problem and our housing stock is committed to people who are already in need. Twelve hundred soldiers from our Scottish regiments, in addition to those made redundant in the Scots Guards, and the other parts of the Services faced with contraction, will make a much greater impact on our population than the same numbers spread across the many millions who live in Southern and Midland England.

But what causes us more concern is the fact that these regiments are still needed. The plans to cut the Scottish Infantry were made when a peaceful new world order seemed round the corner. Eighteen months have passed and that hope has been shattered. The British Army needs our regiments now, and will continue to need them until an era of true peace dawns.

We cannot easily absorb the extra jobs and homeless soldiers who will leave if the amalgamations go through. Britain needs those regiments. We ask you, therefore, on behalf of the Scottish communities that we represent, to Keep Our Scottish Battalions.

Signed ....

On behalf of (Council) ....

All campaigners in the various Regimental areas were now concentrating on ensuring a good turn out in Edinburgh on the 11th December. Posters had been printed and distributed nationally and the sub-committee were meeting regularly in the offices of Citigate in Ainslie Place, Edinburgh. We had also activated supporters to help in Dundee and Perth. All the Royal British Legion Clubs had been circularised with the help of Brigadier Bob Riddle, and we were getting regular mentions on television and local radio. Fred Tattersall of the London and Southern Counties KOSB Association agreed to send out a letter to all his members, advising them of the Rally and Mike MacDonald, an ex-Borderer who manages British Airways Shuttle managed to get posters up at Heathrow airport. The Gordons by now had raised a strong party to come south including Lonnach Pipe Band with their much photographed Drum Major Ian Morrison. Pipe Major David Bunyan had raised a large Border Band despite the fact that Friday 11th December was a working day. I had written to the local press in the Borders asking employers to be sympathetic to supporters asking for the day off, and most were.

The use of the Ross Bandstand in Princes Street Gardens was proving to be difficult with Edinburgh District Council, as girders used in the summer, but dismantled in the winter months were lying on the site where we proposed to parade. The District Council were being less than co-operative, saying we would have to pay a quite ridiculous amount of money to move the girders, which weighed several tons. Councillor Christine Richard, the leader of the Tory Group on the Council did her best, but in the end Charlie Laidlaw gave the story to the press, and within a few hours we had the offer of a crane and a driver to move the girders, which was done for a bottle of whisky courtesy of Bells Islander.

Charlie Laidlaw and I had met the police regarding the Rally some weeks prior to the event, and they were very co-operative and helpful on what as to be a nightmare weekend for them, as the Scottish Fishermen and Scotland United were also holding Rallies. We had hired St Cuthberts Church Hall, adjacent to Kings Stables Road as a base, and a gathering point after the Rally. This Church is well worth a visit to anyone who has not been there, being very attractive and well maintained. It also has the distinction of being the only Church to my knowledge that has served up whisky and beer to supporters of the Infantry.

The Royal Scots had been mustering their supporters and Mike Ashmore had organised leaflets to be distributed around Edinburgh. As at the Galashiels Rally in August we had difficulty in getting a Conservative speaker to maintain our cross party image, but at the 11th hour Charlie Laidlaw managed to get Alasdair Hutton, the former Euro MP to speak, thus completing the platform party of Winne Ewing, John Home-Robertson, Sir David Steel and General MacMillan. All but Strathclyde of the regional and district councils had signed the Declaration of Support, to be handed to the Prime Minister by two KOSB wives, and messages of support from Burgomeisters in Belgium and Holland had been received. Frank Coutts had also written to the principle newspaper in Vlissingen/Flushing enlisting the support of the people of Walchern who had been liberated by The Royal Scots and the KOSB on the 7th November 1944. The Cheshire Regiment, Cheshire Senior Regiment and the Staffordshire Regiment had agreed to send representatives, and the Staffordshire Regiment brought their Regimental Mascot, a Staffordshire Bull

Terrier.

I went up to Edinburgh ahead of the regimental transport leaving Graham Thomson in charge, to assist Charlie Laidlaw and Campbell Graham with last minute arrangements. The police anti-bomb squad had cleared and sealed Princes Street Gardens before my arrival at 9am. This operation included the lifting of drain covers, and the sealing of waste bins and the employment of sniffer dogs. By 9.30 there was a real buzz in Kings Stables Road with Pipers tuning up and drummers rattling their drums. By 10.30 there was a huge assembly of regimental supporters including the large Gordon Highlander contingent who had left Deeside at 5.30am in the dark. Campbell Graham organised the parade into regimental sections in a most humorous manner, interspersing the many pipe bands between regimental groups, with Bunyan's massed Border band leading the parade. The Leith Marching Band had been sent on half an hour before the main parade to encourage the public to come and watch. Major Ken Fraser organised the placing of the Royal British Legion Standards around the Bandstand as they marched in and the various pipe bands facing outwards, towards the regimental supporters. This had the effect of making what was a large Rally look even bigger to impress the media from all over Europe, in Edinburgh for the Summit Conference. General MacMillan gave his best performance to date, and was ably supported by the other speakers. At the conclusion of the speeches the Drum Major of the Lonnach Band, Ian Morrison and some of his Pipers, escorted the two KOSB wives to the Caledonian Hotel where they handed over the Declaration to the Prime Minister.

The Edinburgh Rally achieved its objective of keeping the Campaign in the news. Both television stations carried it on the news, and even *The Times* printed a photograph of Ian Morrison, the bearded Lonnach Drum Major with the caption "Regimental Campaigners come down from the hills", no doubt reinforcing the widely held opinion south of the border that Scots are all bearded, whisky swilling, haggis eating people living in caves in the hills. The Lonnach Pipe Band not content with playing at the Rally went on a walkabout below the Castle, and along Princes Street after the Rally to the delight of the European press men in Edinburgh for the summit. General MacMillan in a letter following the Rally wrote "I doubt if there's been a party like that in St Cuthbert's Church Hall before - and I wonder if there will be again."

Chapter 20

The Christmas Parliamentary Recess 1992

The task of letter writing to MPs continued during the lead-up to Christmas, especially to MPs on the Select Committee who were due to make their second report after the Christmas recess. On the 15th December, *The Times* printed a letter signed by ten former GOCs Scotland which was also printed in *The Scotsman* north of the border. This letter had an important impact on the Campaign, as it preceded the Defence Select Committee's second report which was to prove equally critical of the government's policy. The letter coming only five days after the Edinburgh Rally continued the head of steam we had built up in the press...

Letter to *The Times* 15/12/92
MORE DEMANDS ON ARMY RESOURCES
From General Sir Philip Christison and others:
Sir,

Since August 1991 we, as former General Officers Commanding Scotland, have been expressing our disquiet that the Army will not have enough Infantry battalions to meet its commitments if the full cuts proposed under "Options for Change" went ahead. Since then extra units have been needed in Northern Ireland and Bosnia. Gaps between emergency tours are now only 15 months against a declared target of two years.

The foreign secretary has expressed his belief that further calls on our limited resources will come from Europe and the United Nations. Experience in Northern Ireland shows the folly of planning on any troop reduction there. The Hong Kong scene looks far from settled.

Scottish Members of Parliament are to call on the Defence Secretary on December 17th. They will urge him to review his plans now to reflect the world as it is and not as his advisors wish it to be. When decisions are taken, as surely they must be, to retain more Infantry battalions, we trust that the excellent manning record of the Scottish regiments will be taken into account.

Yours etc

Philip Christison (1947-9)
Derek Lang (1966-9)
Henry Leask (1969-72)
Chandos Blair (1972-6)
David Scott-Barrett (1976-9)
Michael Gow (1979-80)
David Young (1980-2)
Sandy Boswell (1982-5)
Norman Arthur (1985-8)
John MacMillan (1988-91)
c/o 17 Ainslie Place Edinburgh
3 December 13th

As a consequence of the letter to *The Times*, the Admiral of the Fleet Lord Hill Norton writing from the House of Lords on the 29th December to *The Times* wrote. . .

Letter to *The Times* 29/12/92
TIME TO REASSESS FORCES REDUCTIONS
From Admiral of the Fleet, Lord Hill-Norton

Sir,

I warmly agree with General Christison and the other Scottish generals who wrote to you (letter, December 15) about the folly of the reductions in the number of Infantry battalions proposed in Options for Change. Indeed I know of no one in a position to understand these matters who does not agree.

Mr Tom King, when the Treasury persuaded him to publish this ill-judged document, may or may not have understood what its effects would be on our ability to discharge our political-military responsibilities. Be that as it may, his white paper would have been more accurately entitled "Options for Fudge".

Clemenceau may or may not have been right in holding that it was too serious a business for the generals, but what is luminously clear is that the formation of defence policy is too difficult a business for politicians.

We must all hope that, before they take on any more open-ended military commitments, for political reasons, Mr Rifkind will be able to persuade his colleagues that Options for Change should be torn up, and the Chief of Staff invited to decide what the strength of the Army (and indeed, the other services) should be, if the defence and overseas policy of the government is to be successfully supported.

I remain Sir, your obedient servant,

Hill-Norton

House of Lords

Prior to Christmas, Operation Borderer had dispatched Christmas cards to all our contacts at the Ministry of Defence, and Members of Parliament. Colonel Ross Thomson based in Galashiels with the TA and the Cadets, acting quite independently had sent a Christmas card adapted and designed by his wife Pauline, to the Defence Secretary, the Secretary of State for Scotland, and all Members of Parliament. Apart from being particularly apposite, it demonstrated the level of interest and enthusiasm that the campaign was still generating. We knew that Ross felt frustrated by the constraints placed upon him, still being a serving officer, and we had greatly appreciated his behind the scenes help. He personally cleaned all the mess silver prior to our luncheon following the Galashiels Rally.

Chapter 21

The Christmas Meeting with
The Defence Minister
17th December 1992

On the 17th December our Campaign Chairman General Sir John MacMillan in the company of Brigadier John Levey and several MPs met with the Minister of Defence, Malcolm Rifkind, and were able to put further pressure on the government to review matters. The General wrote to us the following day to report on the meeting. . .

18th December 1992
Dear All,

I had a most interesting hour with Malcolm Rifkind yesterday.

Nicky Fairbairn arranged the meeting so that he gave a short introduction and then handed over to me. The other MPs joined in later, but I had the lion's share of the discussion. I had thought I was going to have to take a back seat and only speak when spoken to, so was delighted.

The main point that I think I was successful in making was that running the Army at the pace it is going at the moment will not show in poor morale when people as distinguished as the Secretary of State visit units. It is a high day in their life, and they are probably in a tough spot, and the adrenalin flowing. Short of a disaster, they will put a tremendous face on life. But the pressure shows up when they are in a dull station doing the chores of a depleted garrison, and with half the unit away on the courses they haven't been able to do any other time. And the impact of the present level of operations is dramatically affecting the opportunities to train for the All Arms conflict. John Levey gave me the programme for the 6 Warrior battalions in 1993, and the only one not doing a 6 month tour next year is in Northern Ireland now!

I had a good crack about the value of local links if recruiting is to be maintained, and the effect of change, as shown by the demise of the Cameronians. Scotland's pre-eminence as a recruiting base for the Infantry is likely to last far longer than the amalgamated English regiments will achieve, because we still have the local links.

Nicky pointed our how much more difficult we would find it to meet the numbers needed for the new regiments if names and links are changed. We said Scotland could provide the units he is sure to need, but when he said we couldn't expect him to keep our battalions and disband others that are scheduled to survive I pointed out that the King's Division might yet have to admit that they could not man all their battalions.

Archie Hamilton pointed out that not all operations were bad for training, but I think Malcolm got the message that there is a world of difference between practising driving a Warrior in Bosnia and being ready for a Gulf type engagement, and that is the level of training that has gone for a ball of chalk.

There was a number of other relevant points made by the MPs, ranging from the tradition factor to the important point that damage is already being caused in the regiments earmarked for amalgamation, as recruiting of young Officers becomes harder and applications in all ranks for redundancy come from the people with the gumption to get up and go. The effect of the high proportion of Scottish redundancies from the Army, distorted by the heavy cuts in our Infantry and the particular problems of housing ex-servicemen when they come home, also got a mention.

After a full hour we made the first move to leave, rather then being kicked out, and although Malcolm had said earlier that he thought the Army could still handle the tasks that it was facing with the units at its disposal, and things might get better, if, for instance, Guatemala really did give up its claim to Belize, his final words were that he would ask his officials a number of questions as a result of our discussion. I just wish we were going to be there when they answer them.

The next move is to cash in on the Select Committee report to the best of our ability. The Committee is spitting about the way MoD has fobbed them off with half truths and blatant lies, and I think there is a time bomb being primed there.

To try and get another bite at the cherry John Levey and I have approached MPs who are not Select Committee members to get them to apply for an adjournment debate. I have gone to George Kynoch, and asked him to drum up some Scottish support. I think Patrick Cormack is going to do the same in the South. I understand the more MPs you get, the better the chance of being chosen, and that Patrick Cormack failed over the debate he tried to rustle up on the Defence Estimates early this month. There is no knowing, though, whether you will get selected, and we may have to do some pretty snappy briefing if the debate comes up at short notice. Please keep me posted of any new event or trend that might help in such a briefing.

Yours
John

Chapter 22

The Lead up to the Statement
on Defence on 3rd February 1993

The work done by General MacMillan and John Levey when they gave evidence to the Select Committee on Defence in November, and at their meeting with Malcolm Rifkind in December was beginning to have an effect. MPs understanding of overstretch and too frequent emergency tours was much better and beginning to come through in replies to our letters. The Royal Scots had always maintained that Malcolm Rifkind was not being fully briefed by the Ministry of Defence, and it was clear that General MacMillan and John Levey had done a very good job in briefing him. When Malcolm Rifkind was appointed to Defence, after the General Election, we had made a decision to leave him alone to take stock of his position, and this we had done until late November when we started writing letters to him. We knew the second Select Committee report was going to be very critical of the government position and that it would call for a halt to any further amalgamations, and so it came as a bit of a bombshell when the front page of *The Scotsman* on 15th January 1993 shouted "Rifkind dashes hopes of reprieve for regiments".

The *Scotsman* article went on to say that in an interview, Mr Rifkind had effectively killed off any hopes of a reprieve for the Scottish regiments. They also devoted their editorial to the fact that the Campaign had failed, although not for lack of vigour.

The editorial continued "Tom King's logic was always clear, the eastern threat had receded, warfare had become more technological, and an end was in sight to commitments like Hong Kong and Belize. What was not, and is not, so clear that the right conclusion to draw from this logic is a reduction in the number of Infantry Battalions from 55 to 38. Senior Defence figures have persistently argued that it is not, and, while their resistance is scarcely astonishing, they have managed to persuade a remarkably broad spectrum of opinion to their cause."

Frank Coutts wrote to me on 19th January saying "commiserations on last Friday's *Scotsman* which was a crushing blow. But all is not lost. I have highlighted the loophole. Rifkind is quoted as saying 'the only legitimate debate is about whether there is going to be enough Infantry to meet the Army's requirements over the next few years. If the answer is yes that is the end of the discussion.' Ah! but he didn't go on to say what the outcome would be if the answer were *no*. The Commons Select Committee on Defence has clearly said *no* and the Defence Secretary and the House of Commons must now face that verdict."

On Christmas Eve I went to our local wine shop to pick up some wine and ran into Lord Sanderson of Bowden, who was collecting supplies. He asked me how the Campaign was going and we chatted briefly in the shop. As he had two boxes to carry, I carried one of them for him to his car. It was then that he told me that he had dined with the GOC, Sir Peter Graham, and that it has been realised within government that the Regimental amalgamations were "politically and militarily unacceptable in Scotland, and we are seeking ways of reducing manpower without going ahead with amalgamations". I telephoned Charlie Laidlaw on returning home, and told him of the conversation. Charlie was excited by the news. Because of the Christmas holiday the papers were not printed on Christmas day, so Charlie leaked the conversation to the radio and television news desks.

I was besieged by telephone calls all Christmas Eve, but insisted to all the media that it had been a private conversation between myself and Lord Sanderson, and before using the information they would have to clear it with him. Lord Sanderson naturally denied the content of our conversation, although he admitted that we had talked. Fortunately Grampian Radio interviewed Bill Walker MP (Tayside) and he stated, "I had a conversation with Malcolm Rifkind before Christmas about the regiments. He asked me not to go public before the New Year as things were still under review. I took that to mean the structure proposed for the regiments was no longer viable and could not continue." By Boxing day the telephone lines were buzzing, as this confirmed broadly what Lord Sanderson had told me, and what Charlie had told the media. There was also a rumour that *The Sunday Telegraph* defence correspondent had seen a document confirming plans to announce the cancellation of the amalgamations. On thinking about the conversation with Lord Sanderson, I was sure that he had leaked the information to me deliberately, as it was known he had worked behind the scenes on behalf of the Campaign since "Options for Change" was first announced. During the Christmas holiday, Bill Walker MP started to backtrack on his radio interview, which had also by now been reported in the press.

We took this to mean he had been told to be quiet by Malcolm Rifkind, and gave us further evidence that the matter of the amalgamations was under review. In addition the *Sunday Telegraph* story was somehow suppressed which convinced me beyond all doubt there was something afoot.

Charlie Laidlaw, Willie Turner and myself had been speaking regularly with Ian Bruce, the defence correspondent of *The Herald*. Some of his investigative journalism had been excellent, and he seemed to have a "nose" for when things were about to happen. He had really pushed the boat out with his "exclusive" on December 29th based on my conversation with Lord Sanderson.

It read: "About turn on Scots regiments . . . Threatened four live to fight another day." Ian was convinced that his phone was bugged as was Douglas Robson in Aberdeenshire, so a special number was given to us to use when telephoning Ian. Through one of his contacts he knew that, contrary to usual practise, only two copies of the Select Committee report existed. One copy was with the Commons printer, and the other was with the Committee's own secretariat which MPs had to sign for and read on the premises, before it was locked away in a safe. I spoke to Ian Bruce following the *Scotsman* article and he told me that the Select Committee report was a "damning document", and he understood that the Conservative members on the Committee had to be restrained from demanding the reversal of cuts already made, as well as those to be phased in over the next two years. This news encouraged us greatly, and we were overjoyed when *The Herald* on 27th January carried an exclusive with the headline "MPs set out ambush over Army cuts". Ian revealed that a further batch of redundancy notices were due to be sent out in February, including some of the members of the Cheshire Regiment serving in Bosnia. The provincial press soon latched on, and the Campaign was back on the attack. Because of the suspicion we had regarding our telephone calls, Douglas Robson and I were careful what we repeated on the telephone. Douglas had been convinced that his phone was being interfered with for sometime, and I must admit that on occasions some very strange noises were heard during our calls. My wife Pat, after one particularly peculiar call I had with Douglas, returned to the house after walking the dog bursting with laughter, as she had found a cow scratching itself on our very rural telephone line.

The Mail on Sunday were very active during all of January. Paul Keel phoning regularly to Douglas Robson and myself, and we knew they were working on a major story on Defence. On 24th January they printed two full pages, an article by Paul Keel quoting Major General Peter Martin of the Cheshires who said "when John Major visited our soldiers in Bosnia he said the country should be proud of them. He didn't say that a lot of them would be getting the sack. This uncertainty about whether they have a future in the modern Army is hanging over them while they are out there on duty for the United Nations getting shot at. It really isn't good enough. And I am not alone in thinking so." In addition to Paul Keel's article Rodney Tyler wrote a piece entitled "Analysis" in which he revealed that morale was sinking as Officers protested that the thin red line was getting thinner. The *Mail on Sunday* "Opinion" section stated: "The British Army is coming perilously close to being a modern-day atlas - carrying the troubles of the world on its shoulders. Our armed forces are a credit to this country. They hold one of the keys to our influence and status in the world. They offer excellent value for money. It's time we had a commitment to their future which matched the demands we make of them."

Indications that a rethink of "Options for Change" was taking place was confirmed on 26th January when the Foreign Secretary Douglas Hurd questioned on the situation in Bosnia, stated that Army numbers were under constant review. Tom King also admitted in public "that he had got the Army numbers wrong". Our regular letters to Mr Stainton at the Ministry of Defence had gone unanswered since November, and it was confirmed later, when he wrote following the reprieve of the Regiment, that he was unable to answer the questions. We understood his reluctance to reply to our letters as he had put his head in a noose in June 1992 when he wrote: "the Select Committee on Defence broadly agreed with Options for Change". This letter I copied to John Home-Robertson who replied saying, "I think that Mr Stainton of the Ministry of Defence is taking great liberties in his interpretation of the conclusions of the Select Committee Report, and I may have an opportunity to refer to that fact if I am re-appointed to the Committee when it is re-established shortly." He had also referred publicly to the letter at our Rally in

Galashiels when he described it as "damned impertinence". By the end of January details of the much leaked Select Committee report were being discussed openly by campaigners and the press. It was thought that Defence Secretary Malcolm Rifkind would have to make some sort of statement to take the heat out of the situation.

On Tuesday, 2nd February, Charlie Laidlaw telephoned to say that he had information on very good authority that Malcolm Rifkind would make a statement regarding the regiments the following day about 3.30pm in the House of Commons. There were frantic telephone calls all evening on the 2nd February, with campaigners and pressmen phoning with news. Ian Bruce of *The Herald*, was as usual, well informed, and assured me the Borderers would be saved. Early on the 3rd February we were told that the Colonels of the Royal Scots and The King's Own Scottish Borderers had been told to be available to take telephone calls. The Colonel of The King's Own Scottish Borderers, Brigadier Colin Mattingley could not be reached as he was involved in a meeting in London. When I returned home at lunchtime on the 3rd February, Colonel Clive Fairweather telephoned from his office in Edinburgh Castle to say it was 99% certain we were going to be part of an addback, and to stand by the television broadcast which was live from the House of Commons. At 3.31pm Malcolm Rifkind, the Secretary of State for the Armed Forces, stood up and said: "With permission Madam Speaker, I should like to make a statement about Army manpower." The full text of the Defence Secretary's statement was as follows. . .

ARMY MANPOWER

The Secretary of State for Defence (Mr Malcolm Rifkind):

"With permission, Madam Speaker, I should like to make a statement about Army Manpower.

My Right Hon Friend the Member for Bridgewater (Mr King) set out our plans for Britain's Army for the 1990s in June and July 1991. Those reflected the United Kingdom's leadership of, and substantial contribution to, the new Allied Command Europe Rapid Reaction Corps, as well as the need to provide for the direct defence of the United Kingdom, our responsibilities in our dependent territories and elsewhere and our continued support of the Royal Ulster Constabulary in Northern Ireland. He envisaged at that time that there would be some 116,000 regular personnel in the Army by the mid-1990s. That figure included some 12,000 personnel under training, giving a total trained strength of around 104,000.

Both he and I have repeatedly emphasised the importance we attach to ensuring that the armed forces are able to respond to the demands we place upon them. The requirement to allow suffi-cient leeway to deal with the unexpected was one of the major considerations underpinning the original work on "Options for Change". My predecessor and I have also made clear that we shall keep the position under review and that, should we judge it necessary to look again at planned force levels and the balance between capabilities, we shall do so.

The judgements made in "Options for Change" remain valid. The threat to our national security is much less than it was. Since 1991, however, there have been a number of developments which have added significantly to the commitments that the Army is required to meet at the same time as it is in the process of reorganising. Additional battalions have been deployed to Northern Ireland, and our overall contribution to United Na-tions peacekeeping tasks - in Cyprus, Cambodia, the former republic of Yugoslavia and elsewhere - has almost trebled. The effect of these additional commitments, combined with the disruption caused by the restructuring and drawdown, is placing increasing pressure on individual soldiers and their families. This is something about which many Hon Members have understandably expressed concern. As planning for the Rapid Reaction Corps and other elements of the force structure has been taken forward, a number of requirements for additional manpower have also been identified.

Against that background, I have been considering for a number of months, with my military advisers, the need to adjust the force levels set out by my Right Hon Friend. I have concluded that there is a case for an adjustment in the planned strength of the Army. I am therefore announcing today measures which, together with initiatives already in train, will make available 5,000 additional men and women for the front line units of the field Army.

First, I am announcing that the planned strength of the Army in the mid-1990s should be increased by 3,000 to 119,000. In determining how to use that additional manpower, I have been influenced by two considerations. The first consideration is that it is desirable to bring up to strength a number of units which would otherwise have to be reinforced in order to undertake their peacetime operational commitments; a significant proportion of the additional manpower will be used for that purpose.

The second consideration is that the government attach importance to increasing the emergency tour interval towards the target of 24 months, to which we remain committed. That can best be achieved by revising the number of battalions that will be available in future. I have decided therefore to permit the retention of two further Infantry battalions. There will therefore now be a total of 40 battalions - including two Gurkha - in 1998 compared with 38 previously planned. That will have the effect of increasing the average interval between emergency tours from 15 to 17 months this year and providing an additional margin above 24 months once restructuring is complete, which would make it easier to accommodate any further commitments.

I come now to how the two additional battalions which I have consulted the Chief of the General Staff and my other colleagues on the Army Board of the Defence Council. After considering all the reductions currently under way or planned, it is our unanimous view that the amalgamations of The Cheshire Regiment and The Staffordshire Regiment and of The Royal Scots and The King's Own Scottish Borderers should not now proceed.

The funding for that additional manpower will be met from within the financial provision announced for defence in November 1992 autumn statement. We are at present considering the consequences for the armed forces of the financial position available. Today's announcement will make those decisions more difficult, but I am in no doubt that the need to increase Army manpower is the highest priority currently facing my Department.

This leads to the second area where extra manpower will be released. As well as the increase of 3,000 in the total size of the Army, the development of detailed plans for reorganisation, and the implementation of market testing and other initiatives aimed at improving efficiency should release approximately a further 2,000 personnel, mainly from the support area, over the next few years. Some of that manpower will be available for deployment to field Army units.

While it is important that the armed forces should be large enough to carry out the tasks required of them, manpower is a very expensive resource and I do not believe that it is sensible in terms of the overall defence programme and profile to view their size as permanently fixed. I will continue to keep the long-term strength of the Army under close review in light of changing circumstances. Such circumstances will include any changes to current and foreseeable operational commitments, including the planned withdrawal from Hong Kong. More generally, they will also include further progress with the government's market testing and other initiatives, which should help us to reduce our requirement for service and civilian manpower across the programme. It is also important that senior commanders should have the flexibility to decide on the balance of manpower and other resources that they use to meet the objectives placed on them. Finally, following the publication last year of the open government document on the future use of reserves, we have yet to complete our studies of how best to integrate both regular and volunteer reservists into the post-Options forces structure. That too will have implications for the long-term strength of the Regular Army.

In "Options for Change" we committed ourselves to an Army which is fully manned, properly supported, and well equipped. The decision I have announced today reflects that commitment. I have arrived at this decision only after several months of consideration with my professional military advisers. It represents a small by sensible adjustment to the planned size of the Army that will ensure that it has the flexibility and resilience that it needs to meet the challenges of the 1990s and beyond."

I quite freely admit that there were tears in our eyes as Pat and I listened to him say "it is our unanimous view that amalgamations of the Cheshire Regiment and the Staffordshire Regiment and of the Royal Scots and the King's Own Scottish Borderers should not now proceed." Operation Borderer had been a success, and a huge cheer went up all over the Borders.

During the morning of the 3rd February, Border Television who had got wind of the Defence Secretary's statement, telephoned and asked me if I would go to Carlisle to appear live on the evening news. Radio Tweed who had also been alerted asked me if I would call in on them on my way to Carlisle. This resulted in me cutting the deadline for the news programme very fine. I only had time to dash into the make-up department, before going on live on Border News and Lookaround. It had all been such a rush, and I was so relieved it had gone relatively well, that I forgot to remove my make-up when I left Carlisle. I decided to call in at a local wine shop in Selkirk on my way home, so that we could celebrate the reprieve. I thought the assistant was looking rather intently at me when giving me my change, and it was only when a local wag, in for his half-bottle remarked, "going out tonight are we?" that I realised I still had make-up on, and beat a very hasty retreat to the sanctity of Fountainhead Cottage, and a long list of telephone calls.

On the 9th February I wrote the following letter to Defence Secretary Malcolm Rifkind which, unlike our previous letters was promptly answered by his private secretary, JS Pitt-Brooke.

9th February 1993

Operation Borderer want to place on record our thanks for the huge part you played on behalf of the Royal Scots and The King's Own Scottish Borderers. It was a most courageous decision. We understand from contacts that had it not been for your personal support, it may well have been other regiments reprieved. Our heartfelt thanks; this decision has meant a great deal to the people of Edinburgh and the Borders.

Once a Borderer always a Borderer.

Yours sincerely

WD *Fairgrieve*

Operation Borderer

And the reply from the Ministry of Defence:

12th February 1993

Dear Mr Fairgrieve,

The Secretary of State for Defence has asked me to thank you for your letter of 9th February commenting on his decision not to proceed with the amalgamation of the Royal Scots and the King's Own Scottish Borderers.

The decision was taken to ensure that the Army could meet the commitments placed on it without making unreasonable demands of Army personnel. The Army will now be sufficiently large to meet all of

147

its commitments, and Mr Rifkind is pleased that the King's Own Scottish Borderers will play a part in this, in the future as in the past.

Yours sincerely

John S Pitt-Brooke

Private Secretary

On the 9th February, following Malcolm Rifkind's statement in the House of Commons, The Keep Our Scottish Battalions Committee issued the following press release.

9th February 1993

The government should undertake a full and proper defence review in the light of recommendations contained in the Defence Select Committee's report (Second Report - Britain's Army for the 1990s: Commitments and Resources [HC306]) published today, according to Lt General Sir John MacMillan, former GOC Scotland and chairman of the Keep Our Scottish Battalions Campaign.

Whilst welcoming Defence Secretary Malcolm Rifkind's reprieve of the Royal Scots and the King's Own Scottish Borderers, and the Cheshire and Staffordshire Regiments - which were announced last week - Lt General Sir John MacMillan said they amounted only to "a sticking plaster over the more serious problems of overstretch in the British Infantry."

Brigadier John Levey, chairman of the Save Our Staffords Campaign, said that "the Campaign welcomes the Defence Select Committee report which highlights the very serious problems facing the Army and, in particular, the Infantry.

"The Campaign is, of course, delighted to have had the proposed amalgamations of the Cheshires and Staffords, and the Royal Scots and the King's Own Scottish Borderers, set aside - but that alone will not cure the problem of overcommitment of the Infantry. It but scratches the surface and, in the long term, unless commitments are reduced,

148

further battalions will have to be reprieved."

Lt General Sir John MacMillan also commented: "Unless commitments are reduced, the Army must be given the resources to provide more Infantry battalions.

"When this is recognised, the Ministry of Defence should remember that Scotland is still able to provide fully-manned battalions when other parts of the country cannot.

"The government should now initiate a full and proper defence review in the light of recommendations made by the Defence Select Committee. Such a review would show that the Army must either be given fewer tasks or more infantry units," he said.

Chapter 23

The Freedom March, Galashiels
3rd April 1993

At the end of February I wrote to the Colonel of the Regiment suggesting that some sort of event should be arranged in the Borders to mark the successful conclusion of Operation Borderer. It was decided that the 1st Battalion, with the co-operation of Ettrick and Lauderdale would exercise their rights as "Freemen of Ettrick and Lauderdale" to march through Galashiels with Bayonets fixed, drums beating, and Colours flying. The Regiment were very anxious that this should not be seen as a Victory Parade and strict instructions were issued by Regimental HQ saying that the parade was not an Operation Borderer parade and was being run by the Regiment. There were no banners to be displayed, which rather disappointed our friends from the Gordon Highlanders who wanted to take part. The parade was arranged for the 3rd April which was also Gala Sevens day, and as Inspector Rob Nicholson of Edinburgh and Borders Police remarked "you will never convince the public that it is anything other than a victory parade".

It was a terrific parade attended by ex-Borderers from far and near. The parade was split into two parts. The 1st Battalion led by pipe and military bands, followed by the territorials from Galashiels and Dumfries and Galloway. David Bunyan's volunteer pipe band led the "old and bold" who had turned out in huge

150

numbers. The Selkirk Silver Band also took part, and later played at the reception in the Volunteer Hall. As Inspector Nicholson had predicted it was very much a "victory parade" and the Border public turned out in their thousands to cheer the Battalion. The salute was taken by his Grace the Duke of Buccleuch who was joined on the saluting base by the Colonel of the Regiment, who addressed the parade, and read out a message from our Colonel in Chief Alice Duchess of Gloucester. The reception was held in the Volunteer Hall and really crackled. The safety number of 800 was exceeded by several hundred, as Borderers from all over the country, and abroad, met to celebrate.

The 1st Battalion were entertained to lunch by the Royal British Legion Club, and the District Council, and the hotels and public houses of Galashiels were filled by Borderers. It was a day never to be forgotten, and many a tear was shed. The pipe and military bands played at Netherdale prior to the Sevens, in which a team representing 1 Battalion KOSB took part, due to the late withdrawal of the Irish Wolfhounds. At the conclusion of the reception in the Volunteer Hall Operation Borderer presented a hand carved slate of the Regimental Badge to Lt Colonel John Kirkwood, Officer commanding 1 Bn KOSB.

The slate had been carved by Martin Reilly a Perthshire stone-carver and represented 400 hours work. The slate will eventually be hung in the Museum at Berwick.

On the 21st May Willie Turner and myself were honoured to be presented with a silver quaich inscribed "A Regiment Saved", at an Officers Club dinner in Ednam House Kelso, by the Colonel of the Regiment. Never had our regimental saying "Once a Borderer always a Borderer" been more relevant.